YOU WILL LIVE AGAIN!

plus
Hypnosis and Group Regression
and Actual Case Histories, including:
- The Rebirth of a Civil War Victim
- Bridey Murphy Revisited
- The Man Who Returned as His Grandson
- The Mystery of Naomi Henry

"To those who read this book in an open-minded spirit of inquiry, I can promise a most fascinating series of adventures."

—Brad Steiger

YOU
WILL
LIVE
AGAIN

BRAD STEIGER

A Dell/Confucian Book

Published by

Dell Publishing Co. Inc.
1 Dag Hammarskjold Plaza
New York, New York 10017

and

The Confucian Press, Inc.

Dell ® TM 681510, Dell Publishing Co. Inc.
Printed in the United States of America

ISBN: 0-440-09775-4

First Dell printing—April 1978

Published by arrangement with
Brad Steiger

I wish to acknowledge the cooperation and assistance of a number of men and women whose love and helping hands made my work so much easier: Dick Sutphen, Sutphen Past Life and Future Freedom Seminars, P.O. Box 4276, Scottsdale, AZ 85258; Deon Frey Scudamore, Deon's ESP Center, Box 3845, Merchandise Mart, Chicago, IL 60654; Shad Helmstetter, Metasource Research Institute, P.O. Box 4817, Scottsdale, AZ 85258; Rt. Rev. Kingdon L. Brown, Desert Shadows Church, 6508 East Cactus Road, Scottsdale, AZ 85254; Susan Harris, *The Psychic Gazette,* P.O. Box 2145, Scottsdale, AZ 85252; my late friend and coresearcher, Loring G. Williams; and my own inspiration, my own guru, my wife, Francie, STARBIRTH, 7500 East Butherus Drive, Suite N, Scottsdale, AZ 85260.

YOU
WILL
LIVE
AGAIN

CHAPTER ONE:
YOU WILL LIVE AGAIN!

I became a believer in the survival of the human spirit at the age of eleven. Belief is a subjective kind of knowing, and one need not accept my experience as valid for his own reality. I can understand that position. After all, it took my own death to convince me that the soul is imperishable.

I had a fleeting memory of losing my balance, falling off the tractor, and sprawling into the path of the farm implement with its whirling blades. There was pain as the machine's left tire mashed my upper body, shock as the blades clutched at my head and cut deeply into my flesh and skull. My world was the color of blood.

Then I was floating about forty feet off the ground, looking down on a tractor and farm implement somehow brought under control by my seven-year-old sister, June. I was concerned, yet becoming more detached about such matters by the moment. I seemed strangely unmoved by the scene beneath me. It seemed of only mild importance to me that an eleven-year-old boy was dying on a field in the state of Iowa. I seemed to be an orangish-colored ball, intent on soaring to the sun. I felt a blissful euphoria; and at the same time, a marvelous sense of Oneness with All That Is.

I was aware of my father, shocked and in tears, carrying my body away. I seemed to be in my father's arms, bleeding, mangled, dying; and at the same time I was above us, watching the action as a detached observer.

I thought of my mother; and instantly I seemed to be beside her as she labored in the kitchen, as yet unaware of my accident. I thought of the friends with whom I planned to see the Roy Rogers-Gene Autrey double-feature that night, and I was immediately observing them as they worked with their fathers on their own farms. I seemed also to be at One with Time and Space. I did not really want to return to that battered and bloody body, but it seemed that there were things to do that lay ahead that were much more important than attending cowboy movies.

In the August 12, 1973 issue of the *National Enquirer,* our former family physician, Dr. Cloyce A. Newman, now living in Homestead, Florida, was interviewed about the accident that had taken place twenty-six years before. Dr. Newman told how he had had me rushed by car to a hospital in Des Moines, about 140 miles away: "He was very seriously injured and on the verge of death. We managed to get him to a specialist and it saved his life."

I was in and out of the body during those 140 miles, and I did not really come back with any real intention of staying in the mangled mess that was me until the surgery was about to begin. At that point, it seemed as though some energy insisted that I return to my body to cooperate in the medical procedure which was about to begin. I came back with such force that I sat up, shouted, and knocked an intern off-balance. I began to struggle against the restraining hands of the doctors and nurses, and it took the calming words of a Roman Catholic sister to pacify me until the anesthesia could take effect.

From the perspective of my now forty-one years, I can see that my experience of pseudo-death at the age of eleven was a most fortunate one. Certainly one of the Big Questions that every thinking man and woman eventually asks himself or herself is, "Is there life after death?" And I had that eternal puzzler answered in the affirmative for me before I entered my teens. Yes, there is an essential part of us, most commonly referred to as the soul, that does survive physical death.

But what of the afterlife? Angels and harps in a cloudlike Heaven? Flames and pitchforks in a scalding Hell? A blissfully stagnant Limbo?

The popular acceptance of the work of Chicago psychologist Dr. Elisabeth Kübler-Ross has recently brought sharp scientific focus to bear on the question of what happens to man after the experience of physical death. In her book, *Death, The Final Stage of Growth,* Dr. Kübler-Ross declares that "beyond a shadow of a doubt, there is life after death." Far from an evangelical tract, Dr. Kübler-Ross's volume is actually a textbook which is based on more than a thousand interviews with terminally ill persons, many of whom had recovered from pseudo-deaths similar to the one which I experienced. They, too, described the sensation of floating above their own bodies and being able to transcend the accepted physical limitations of Time and Space. Nearly all told of that same sense of euphoria and peace, and many had been confronted by spirit beings who told them that it was not yet time for them to make the final transition to the other side.

When the dying do accomplish that ultimate change between worlds, according to Dr. Kübler-Ross's observations, they are ". . . at peace; they are fully awake; when they float out of their bodies they are without

fear, pain, or anxiety; and they have a sense of whole-
ness."

Dr. Raymond Moody discovered an enormous number of similar reports when he became curious about
what happened to patients in the period of time in which
they "died" before being revived and returned to life
through medical treatment. After interviewing many
men and women who had had such experiences, Dr.
Moody found what Dr. Kübler-Ross and many previous
researchers (such as Dr. Karlis Osis of the American
Society for Psychical Research) had discovered:

• The resurrected hear a loud, uncomfortable ringing
or buzzing sound.

• They have the sensation of moving rapidly through
a long, dark tunnel before "popping" outside of their
physical bodies. If they are in hospital rooms or other
enclosures, they often float near the ceiling and watch
the medical teams attempting to revive their physical
bodies.

• Many reported their life literally "flashing" before
their eyes.

• They are often welcomed to the other world by
previously deceased friends or relatives.

• Whether or not they are of a "churched" background, they often report an encounter with a brilliant,
intense white light that has the form of an angel, a
guide, a teacher, or a Christ-figure.

Dr. Moody, who is both a medical doctor and the
holder of a doctorate in philosophy, emphasizes that he
is not attempting to "sell" a point of view; but he freely
confesses that after talking with hundreds of men and
women who have had the pseudo-death experience, he
personally does not doubt that there is survival of
bodily death.

"I'm not drawing that conclusion as a scientist," he is quick to add. "In fact, I don't think that there will be a definite proof of life after death in the strict sense. I believe this is more a matter of faith. After all my research and interviews, I'm personally a believer."

Can physical proof of survival exist in those men and women who claim to remember past lives? Can belief be supported by an examination of the evidence, both subjective and objective, that certain individuals have incarnated before on Earth? If one survives physical death, may not reincarnation be at least one of the forms in which that survival expresses itself?

Hypotist–psychical–researcher Dick Sutphen, who conducts workshops and seminars in hypnotic regression in what would seem to be former lives, asserts that ". . . the ultimate value of regression to many people is that they may become aware of the cause of some major problem in their life and therefore can begin to release the cause and therefore the problem."

In Sutphen's world view, each incarnation is for the purpose of learning and loving and in transcending present levels of knowledge and love. "We learn in this lifetime and graduate into the next one," he remarks. "If we don't learn a particular lesson, we must start all over again in a subsequent lifetime.

"There is absolutely no doubt in my mind that men and women together in this lifetime have been together before. Even if their involvement is only a brief affair, there was a reason why they needed to touch again. Today's situation could be explained by what happened in a past life. Or, to put it another way, because of 'cause and effect,' which is Karma."

Sutphen argues that the chain of cause and effect would trace everything that has ever happened in the universe back to some original cause. When the effect is felt in man, the cause was set in motion in the mind. The effects being felt now, both positive and negative, are the results of causes from this lifetime or from previous lifetimes.

One's entire life—his mental state, his health, his relationships with others, the material gains he may or may not make—are all effects which have been set in motion by causes to be found somewhere in one's background, in this life or in previous ones. "Karma," according to Sutphen, "is totally just." The laws of compensation will eventually balance each individual Soul as it progresses toward God.

Psychologist and hypnotherapist Dr. Edith Fiore has attended a number of the Sutphen seminars and has appraised Dick as "an excellent, very sincere hypnotist and a very knowledgeable person." Dr. Fiore has been able to overcome some of her scientific skepticism toward reincarnation: "There are just too many cases of people who have gone through regression and come up with valid information. I've had patients with obesity problems who were regressed to former lifetimes where they starved to death. As soon as they relived the experience, they started to lose weight."

Could such "past-life recalls" actually be imaginary projections on the part of the patient? "It doesn't really matter whether it's fantasy or reality," Dr. Fiore remarked. "The important thing is that the person gets well."

In her monthly column in the April 1977 issue of *Human Behavior* magazine, Eleanor Links Hoover presented an interesting prediction concerning public acceptance of reincarnation in the Western world: "It is coming at us from all sides now—new evidence of life after death. The deluge, in fact, is so heavy, some people believe that 10 years from now, the idea of reincarnation will be just as acceptable as acupuncture or hypnosis stands today."

In their May issue, *Human Behavior* cited the research of psychiatrist Reima Kampman of the University of Oulu in Finland which indicates that people who are able to display multiple personalities or alleged past lives under hypnosis are actually healthier than those who cannot.

According to *Human Behavior:*

> One of Kampman's subjects, a 20-year-old woman, revealed eight different personalities in progressive chronological order, ranging from a young woman who lived in Russia during the Bolshevik revolution . . . to an 18th-century titled English lady . . . to a girl named Bessina who said she lived in Babylonia. . . . Contrary to what the established psychiatric literature would lead one to believe, these were not troubled minds on the verge of fragmentation. Compared with those who could not rise to the hypnotist's challenge, the multiple-personality group had greater stress tolerance, more adaptability and far less guilt. Internal identity diffusion, a neurotic quality defined as the discrepancy between what one feels about oneself and how one feels that others perceive one, was also greater in the nonresponsive group.
>
> Kampman suggests that in the ego-threatening situation induced by the hypnotist's request for other personalities, only the healthy can afford to respond creatively: "Creating multiple personalities is evidence of a highly specialized ability of

the personality to extricate itself adaptively by a deep regression from the conflict situation created by the hypnotist" [says Dr. Kampman].

If it is suggested that the "other lives" secured by a hypnotist might be "evidence of a highly specialized ability of the personality to extricate itself adaptively" from a conflict situation, and nothing more, can it also be theorized that what would seem to be persistent memories of previous lifetimes are also psychological mechanisms of the personality seeking to extricate itself from conflict situations created by the hostile environment in which it may find itself?

Early in 1977, an eminent British psychiatrist announced that his research into the claims made by a patient that she remembered a former lifetime had convinced him that reincarnation is a fact. What is more, the psychiatrist now believes that he, himself, has lived four previous lifetimes.

Dr. Arthur Guirdham, former chief psychiatrist for the British government's National Health Service at Bath, told investigative journalist Alan Markfield that his analysis of the case proved to his satisfaction that both he and the woman patient had been members of a persecuted religious cult in thirteenth-century France. The patient, whom he refers to as "Mrs. Smith" to protect her anonymity, first came to him in 1962, complaining of violent nightmares.

The nightmares she suffered were always of her lying on a floor in a room. A man would enter the room from the outside. She had no precise recollection of what was going to happen, but the expectation of some approaching event had her terrified. Soon after she had come to Dr. Guirdham, the nightmares stopped. Then

Mrs. Smith began to tell him of her memories of a past life.

At first the psychiatrist was bemused by her alleged recollections of her life as a member of the Cathar religious sect. She told him of her sweetheart in that life, Rogiet, a blue-robbed priest of the Cathars. She provided the names of many men and women who had been connected with the group.

As involved as her so-called memories were becoming, Dr. Guirdham remained professionally aloof from the tales until Mrs. Smith stunned him by revealing her conviction that he had been Rogiet, her lover, more than 700 years ago.

Although not openly accepting Mrs. Smith's claims, Dr. Guirdham was intrigued enough to contact a noted French historian, Professor René Nelli, and to request that he conduct a special investigation of the information which she was providing. Professor Nelli later admitted that he at first believed the whole story to be a "lot of noise." But now, after fifteen years of research, he believes "it is true."

Professor Nelli is a faculty member at Toulouse University in France and an authority on thirteenth-century French history. Each time that Dr. Guirdham relayed a bit of information regarding the Cathars, Professor Nelli's search of the ancient records of the Inquisition bore another matching piece of substantiating evidence.

Clinching the argument for Professor Nelli's initial skepticism was Mrs. Smith's insistence that the Cathar priests wore blue robes.

For centuries, scholars had maintained that the French heretics known as the Cathars wore black robes. Mrs. Smith, however, had insisted that the robes of the Cathars were a dark navy blue. Professor Nelli's research found that Mrs. Smith's "memories" were more accurate than the previous scholastic consensus.

The data allegedly dredged up from Mrs. Smith's memories of a former lifetime are not readily available. The members of the Cathar heretical sect, their characters and descriptions, are not to be found in the kind of history book to which one would have easy access in the typical library. Even scholarly tomes on church history carry scant information about the individual members of the Cathar heresy. The only volumes which can substantiate Mrs. Smith's revelations are dusty, ancient records, written in a language which she cannot read or understand.

Dr. Guirdham told Markfield that his experience with Mrs. Smith not only convinced him of her past life, but of his own prior existences. He admitted that he eventually came to have an awareness of his life as Rogiet, as well as three other previous lifetimes—"a servant girl in fourth-century Italy, a priest in seventh-century Britain, and a sailor in nineteenth-century France."

A serious discussion of reincarnation in this era of space-age skepticism toward any aspect of man that cannot be distilled and dissected through the laboratory process is very likely to bring about raised eyebrows in certain social circles. But if Eleanor Links Hoover is correct in her assertion in *Human Behavior* that the "deluge" of evidence for life after death is beginning to make an appreciable dent in the iron-sided spiritual cynicism of the general scientific community, then perhaps the vast amount of empirical evidence supporting reincarnation will not languish forever unrecognized.

This book came into being because of my acquaintance with several cases suggestive of reincarnation that seem to be so extensively documented that any error of judgment on the part of the investigators would appear to be highly unlikely.

As I stated earlier, at the age of eleven I had confirmed for me the validity of spiritual man (i.e., that man and mind are something other than physical things), but at the beginning of my research my entire intellectual, emotional, and religious bias was *against* reincarnation.

The majority of the Western world shares my former prejudices. An Oriental friend of mine once told me that, in his estimation, Western man's refusal to consider the tenets of reincarnation was the major barrier preventing a greater understanding and harmony between Judeo-Christian theology and the religious doctrines of the Orient.

What factors led me to continue to research a subject toward which I had for so long held a prejudgment?

Because of an irritating number of cases that cry out in very articulate and demanding voices to be more carefully studied and understood.

Because of the case histories that held up under the most exacting documentation and examination.

Because of the impressive number of great minds who, through the ages, have professed their acceptance of reincarnation as reality.

And because I, as so many others, have had those strange, ostensible memories of what seem to be past lives—memories so vivid that it would seem that they would have to be more than just psychodramas produced by the brain's dream machinery . . . memories so powerful that if they be but pseudo-memories, then they must be the product of some as yet unnamed power of the unconscious, the reception of telepathic impulses from incarnate or disincarnate beings, or the genetically transferred memory of a forgotten ancestor. And when one has worked himself into an intellectual *cul-de-sac* with each of the alternative explanations, there always remains the possibility that he is actually recalling a past life.

In my opinion, it would not seriously impair the mental processes of even the most rigid materialist to consider that man may be more than flesh and blood, that the essential self may continue to exist without brute matter.

Nor would it upset the chemicals bubbling in the test tubes or the theorems on the physics classroom walls to assert with Johann Wolfgang Goethe, the great German dramatist and poet: "The thought of death leaves me unmoved, since I am convinced that our soul is indestructible, something which progresses perpetually from infinitude to the endless."

Goethe was convinced that the soul inhabited those bodies best fitted to its inherent nature, wandering from one to the other, forcing the flesh to adapt itself without choice. Goethe was a great believer in reincarnation, and he once exclaimed to Charlotte Von Stein that in some previous existence she had been either his sister or his wife.

Goethe believed that he would live again, just as he had lived before.

To those who read this book in an open-minded spirit of inquiry, I can promise a most fascinating series of adventures. Then, when all the evidence has been presented, each reader must weigh the various testimonies and serve as his own judge and jury as to their validity and their truth in his own reality.

You may consider the evidence inconclusive as yet and decide to pursue further the matter with a mind that is no longer rigidly closed to investigations of unorthodox subjects.

On the other hand, you may agree with thousands of men and women who will not hesitate to exclaim: "You will live again!"

CHAPTER TWO:
EXPLORING THE MYSTERY
OF REINCARNATION

"I have always had this very strange recurring dream. I see myself as a cowboy during a trail drive. It must be sometime after the Civil War because some of the men have on battered military hats and high cavalry boots. There is an argument about whether the men should rustle the herd from the owner. I defend the rancher, tell the men that they're crazy to think of stealing. One of the men pulls a revolver and shoots me in the chest. I can feel that slug burn; I can smell gunpowder and cattle; I can see jagged streaks of lightning scratching the dark sky; I can hear the excited chatter of the men get farther and farther away as I lie there dying. Then I wake up, but it has all been so real! Am I actually remembering how I died in a former life?"

"My husband and I went to Mexico last summer. It was something that I had always wanted to do, ever since I was just a little girl. We saw all the things *touristas* are supposed to see; then, on a peculiar compulsion, I asked my husband to turn off on a side road. We had been strongly advised to keep to the main routes, but I had an unquenchable desire to take this particular road. After we had driven a few miles, we came to an obscure little village. It was dirty, unattractive, but I knew that village. It sounds crazy to say it, but I felt that I had lived there before. I knew the arrangement of the town square: I knew the path that led to the lake; and most peculiar of all, I felt a great feeling of warmth toward a withered old couple sunning themselves outside their hut. I actually felt as though they might have been my parents when I lived in that village during a former incarnation."

"When I first met Sarah, I felt that I had known her before. After we had dated for a while, she admitted that she had experienced that same sort of feeling toward me. Just for fun, we checked all the places we had lived as kids or traveled through on vacation trips, but we had never come within a thousand miles of each other before we met. The weirdest part is that I feel that we've lived together before, maybe as man and wife, maybe as brother and sister. We plan to be married soon. What else can we do? It seems as though we have always been together."

Have you, as have my three correspondents quoted above, ever asked yourself, "Have I lived before?"

Have you ever walked down a street in a strange city and been overwhelmed with the sudden familiarity of its shop windows, sidewalks, and store fronts?

Have you ever seemed to experience the arousal of some long-forgotten memory when you lay at ease with a completely tranquil mind?

Or has a hidden memory ever been stimulated by witnessing a dramatic reenactment of some scene from the past?

In an earlier work, I related the story of an eighteen-year-old typist, Miss Dorothy Jordan of Belfast, Ireland, who claimed to have recalled a past life while watching a movie in Liverpool, England.

The theater seemed to become unnaturally dark, and an almost eerie silence enveloped the viewers of Tudor Rose, as the condemned Lady Jane Grey was led to the masked executioner.

As Lady Jane bent her head to the chopping block, a hysterical scream pierced the hush. Silhouetted against the screen was a young woman, waving her arms and shouting: "It's all wrong, all wrong! I know; I was at the execution!"

The year was 1936, and even the poorest student of history in the audience could estimate that an eyewitness to the execution of Lady Jane would have to be pushing four hundred!

The distraught girl fell in a faint, and ushers carried her to the lobby. When revived, Dorothy Jordan told a remarkable story to a reporter for the Empire News. According to the young typist, she had been transported back to another era while she sat watching the film.

When the screen flashed Lady Jane Grey waving through the tower window to her husband, Lord Guilford Dudley, on his way to his own execution, Miss Jordon realized that this was wrong. She knew the room well, and it was impossible to look out of the window!

It was during the execution scene that she first realized she had been Lady Jane's lady-in-waiting! She saw many things in the movie that did not agree with the facts. She had a vivid impression of the executioner, particularly the broad black bands around his wrists. When Lady Jane first saw him, Miss Jordan recalls that she shuddered and clung to her. Then Lady Jane knelt to the block. They lifted her curls . . . and Miss Jordan saw no more. Apparently she fainted.

When she regained consciousness, the surroundings

seemed strange. She was amazed to find herself not in Tudor dress. She is absolutely convinced that the execution happened just as she said.

The reporter from the *Empire News* stated that Miss Jordan appeared to be frank, intelligent, and far from flighty. Upon investigation, it was learned that Miss Jordan had never displayed any particular interest in history and had no knowledge of the various theories of reincarnation.

If we choose to believe the earnest Miss Jordan and the investigation of the *Empire News,* then we will assess this case as an instance in which a young Irishwoman was prompted into reliving the memory of an execution which took place on Tower Hill, London, in 1554.

The whole proposition becomes less laughable if we admit that, at one time or another, we have all felt familiarity in new surroundings, discovered an old house that evoked strange emotions, or had the *déjà vu* experience of feeling "that's happened to me before." But is the "sense of the already known," as it is called in parapsychology, reincarnation?

Could it not be another manifestation of extrasensory perception, the powers that are man's very own?

Could it not be genetic memory, inherited flashes of memories transferred through our ancestors' genes, just like the color of our hair and the size of our brains?

Not too many years ago, a farmer in Wurttemberg, Germany, claimed that he could draw plans of primitive edifices that had been erected on stakes in the marshy Federsee district, many centuries ago.

Taking a bold gamble for orthodox men of science, archeologists began excavation on the basis of the farmer's drawings. It was discovered that the man had hardly missed a thing. Even a hearth marked in one site was exactly where he had indicated that it would be.

When the archeologists returned to question the farmer in order to learn more about the source of his information, the man unhesitatingly told them that he had lived in the primitive lake dwellings during their early habitation.

Reincarnation or genetic memory?

Or what about the actual possession of the living by the dead?

A former Nazi lieutenant who had been stationed in occupied France during World War II gave a newspaper this enigmatic personal memoir.

He had received orders to establish quarters in an obscure Rhone Valley village. Immediately upon arrival, the lieutenant was seized by the bizarre sensation that this remote village was not so foreign to him after all. As he strolled past a schoolhouse, he suddenly had a clear and nostalgic memory of toiling at its cramped wooden desks. In the same puzzling flash of recollection, he remembered his parental home at the back of a small, dingy confectionary shop.

The young German officer traced a boyhood path that lay somewhere in subconscious memory patterns. The elderly woman who opened the creaking door of the shabby house blinked at him in bewilderment as he tried to communicate with the aid of a simplified French-German dictionary.

"There is a small alcove in this house," he managed in his broken French. "It has a small brown cupboard filled with many toys. A small, broken rocking horse stands beside a large stuffed dog. . . ."

The French woman was dumbfounded at first; then she became a little frightened. How could a German officer, a stranger to their village, describe an upstairs room that he had never seen?

The lieutenant insisted on confirming his description, and, trembling with doubt and distrust, the old Frenchwoman led him to the room, where, just as he had said, there stood a cupboard full of toys and a rocking horse near a stuffed dog.

Her eyes glistening with tears, the Frenchwoman told the German officer that twenty-one years earlier her little nine-year-old son had died. In respect of his memory, she rarely entered the room and had left all of his toys scattered where he had last played with them.

"On what date did your son die?" the young officer asked, his voice trembling with excitement.

"Why," she hesitated, "on February 8th."

"That's my birthday," the lieutenant whispered solemnly.

Had the little French boy been reborn as a German? What strange odyssey had brought the boy back to his home village in the person of an invading officer? Or had the young lieutenant been temporarily possessed by the restless soul of the French boy? In the view of modern parapsychology, something of this sort could have been accomplished by the telepathic reception of a discarnate memory pattern.

There are always plenty of such tales in circulation as that of the young German lieutenant, and some must be taken as embellished or completely imaginary anecdotes conjured up by barroom orators, bored housewives, or "true believers." However, there do exist many carefully investigated and thoroughly documented case studies of disturbingly well-founded claims of reincarnation.

* * *

I find the extrasensory hypothesis useful in explaining many cases suggestive of reincarnation, however. Take, for example, the well-attested-to phenomenon of retrocognition, the "psi" experience wherein one perceives a scene from the past and thereby derives information about a past event which he could not have acquired through normal means.

It seems to me that retrocognition could account for such an experience as the businessman who felt himself an Indian while camping with his boy scouts. Perhaps he perceived a scene from the past when Indians did indeed lie sleeping outside of Indian Cave. As he lay there in a semi-trancelike state, some part of his subconscious may have dramatized the incident to include him as a character within the scene instead of being merely the percipient.

To illustrate with an example, we have all had the experience of incorporating the ringing of the alarm clock into our dreams. Tickle the foot of a sleeper and his dream machinery may transform that sensation into the caress of a lovely maid or the slither of a deadly reptile, depending upon some unknown whim of the subconscious.

A young student who so stubbornly insisted that a room lay beyond a stone wall in a German castle may have been sensitive to certain vibrations in the psychic ether and have "seen" through the stone via retrocognition. To offer another ESP-oriented explanation, the student may have clairvoyantly perceived the information of the hidden room from either an ancient book in the curator's office or from the forgotten memories of the curator himself.

Admittedly, the ESP hypothesis is quite unsatisfactory in explaining many of the documented cases with which we have dealt in this book, but by the same token one should not accept every strange flash of "memory" as proof of reincarnation. An unfamiliar room may seem to evoke hidden memories because of its own peculiar atmosphere or because scenes of violent emotional impact have been enacted within its walls. An old stone ax may seem to trigger a flood of memories because of a latent psychometric talent on the part of the individual who touches its surface. But in each of these ESP-induced experiences, the percipient is observing, not remembering.

It seems to me that it was ESP at work rather than a manifestation of reincarnation in this case quoted by Rev. Leslie D. Weatherhead in his *The Case of Reincarnation*.

According to Rev. Weatherhead, in October of 1959, he received a letter from a woman who had a university degree in science but who had had no interest in matters of a psychic nature until after her son's early death. The woman tells of a number of unusual experiences which her son David had during his brief life-span.

"From four years he spoke of an invisible playmate —whom he called his Little Princess. In any difficulty, he would say: 'I must ask my Little Princess.' "

Rev. Weatherhead's correspondent says that she and her husband identified the invisible visiting royalty with her husband's ancestors ". . . and do indeed believe he could see and hear her."

At age seven, according to the woman, David accompanied her to Rome to visit her grandmother, who stayed in Italy a great deal. For an afternoon's outing, the woman and her son accompanied a noted archeologist to view a recently excavated Roman villa on the outskirts of Naples.

From the moment they reached the excavation, David became very emotional and excited and ran about the ruins until he came to a Roman bath engraved with the signs of the Zodiac.

"Here's our bath, and our tiles—mine had a bull on it and the fish was Marcus," the boy shouted excitedly.

"As he said the name 'Marcus,' " the woman writes, "he burst into floods of tears and called out: 'Take me away—it was all so terrible, I can't bear it.' "

Another of David's strange experiences took place when he and his parents were visiting some caves in Guernsey, which had been used at one time as prisons for French soldiers. The boy began to tap on the walls of the cave and told his parents that there was yet another cave where a young prisoner had been walled in.

David told his skeptics that he had "watched it being done."

The authorities denied the existence of such a cave and the perpetration of such an act.

Then David gave the name of the prisoner, and his parents insisted upon a closer examination of the records by the authorities.

"Eventually, steps were taken and the walls were tapped for any thin place which could have been the outline of a door. The door was found; it had been bricked up. Stretched out on the floor was the skeleton of a man. When the archives were searched, the name David had given was correct."

When David was fourteen, his mother accompanied him to look at some new mummies which had been acquired by the British Museum. His mother felt she would be asking for yet another of David's flights into the unknown, but, to her surprise, her son appeared quite calm.

His calm, it appears, was deceptive. After he had

peered inside a sarcophagus, David complained that there should have been three initials on the underside of the case.

His mother asked him if he could draw the initials, and David made three birds on his note pad.

"That was my name," he told her, "but you weren't there then. I was a kind of inspector; I had to mark the coffins if they were satisfactory."

Rev. Weatherhead concludes that such strange happenings have "no adequate interpretation other than that of reincarnation."

It seems much more likely to me that young David was an exceptionally gifted clairvoyant. Such people as Peter Hurkos, Croiset, and my good friend John Pendragon have the extraordinary talent of being able to hold scarves, watches, rings, letters, and other items and thereupon being able to recite episodes of the owner's past, present, and, sometimes, his future.

Such emotion-charged places and objects as an ancient Roman villa, a prison cave, and an Egyptian mummy would seem to be powerful broadcasters to the sensitive psyche of a young clairvoyant. Again, perhaps because of his youth and his inability to understand his ESP talents, David may have projected himself into the impression which he perceived when he came into contact with certain places and things. When such an exceptionally talented clairvoyant as Great Britain's John Pendragon receives emanations from an object or letter, he perceives the impressions of his "psychic screen," almost as if he were watching a television drama unfold. Only under the most unusual of circumstances would a clairvoyant feel himself caught up in the impressions or feel himself a part of the drama.

Another strike which I would call on the interpretation of David's experiences as being suggestive of reincarnation is the matter of the great coincidence of the young man happening to encounter such widely separated locales for his former lives in his own brief life-span.

It would seem to me to be stretching the laws of chance a bit far to consider that a young boy from London could happen to arrive in Naples just as his former villa was being excavated, tour the caves in Guernsey where he had served either as guard or prisoner, and happen to come into contact with the one sarcophagus among thousands that contained the bandaged earthly shell of a former life. No, it seems much more realistic to suppose that David and his parents were unaware of the fact that he was possessed of a great talent for psychometry.

ESP, then, in this writer's opinion, may account for many alleged cases of reincarnation. One little-understood phenomenon may not be used to explain away the existence of another, however, and extrasensory perception as a general hypothesis to account for all cases suggestive of reincarnation, admittedly, does not stand the test.

CHAPTER THREE:
THE REBIRTH OF
A CIVIL WAR VICTIM

One of the most thoroughly documented and well-researched cases suggestive of reincarnation in recent years was published in the December 1966 issue of *Fate.* The article, "Reincarnation of a Civil War Victim," described the hypnotically induced regression of a New Hampshire high school boy to his life as a farmer in Jefferson, North Carolina, during the period of 1840 to 1863.

The author of the piece, Loring G. Williams, was a high school teacher who had developed a reputation for hypnotic prowess. "Bill" has often been called upon to provide entertainment for local fund-raising drives; and, as a member of the Keene State College Psychic Research Society, he has participated in several investigations into the nature of psychic phenomena.

I contacted Bill Williams and told him of my proposed book on reincarnation.

"I'll help you all I can," William said generously. "Some new material has developed since the *Fate* article appeared. For one thing, the boy has recalled additional lives."

Williams told me that it would take him quite a while to make transcripts of all the tape recordings, but he promised to provide me with material just as soon as he could.

In much less time than I expected, a large packet of materials arrived from Williams. He had worked overtime to get the information to me as quickly as possible. Briefly, here is the story of "Jonathan" as it was reported in *Fate*.

George Field, a fifteen-year-old neighbor of Williams, decided one evening to sit in on the weekly sessions which the teacher-hypnotist had been holding in his home. During these meetings, Williams would regress volunteers in the hope that he might find a subject whose story could be checked.

Such a search is not an easy one. As Williams put it, many subjects when regressed are hazy about details. They cannot remember their full names or their parents' names, are not sure where they lived, and are unable to give other details that would be needed to check a story. Others, though they may go into vivid detail, describe an existence so long ago, or in so remote a place, that checking is out of the question. Then along came George.

George Field proved to be an ideal subject for hypnosis. He went easily into trance and was amenable to hypnotic suggestion. Within a short time, George was describing a past existence which had taken place in North Carolina at a point in history which would be near enough to check out.

While in deep hypnotic trance, the New Hampshire teen-ager "remembered" a life as "Jonathan Powell." He recalled that his father's name had been Willard and that his paternal grandmother was named Mary. He could not remember the name of his mother.

According to "Jonathan," his father worked a small farm and labored in the nearby tin mine. The family were Quakers, ministered to by a traveling parson

named Brown. Mr. Brown lived in the "villie" of
Jefferson in Ashe County.

Williams continued to move George-Jonathan forward and backward in the time sequence of his lifetime. As the boy spoke, a tape recorder caught every
word so that, if possible, Williams could substantiate the
physical existence of Jonathan Powell.

Finally, the hypnotist took Jonathan up to his last
day in that incarnation. When Williams asked the
personality what he was doing, Jonathan replied that
he was busy loading potatoes for those "damn Yankee
soldiers."

According to Jonathan, the soldiers were willing to
pay only a few cents a bushel for the crop which he
had worked so hard to harvest. He cursed the men in
their gray uniforms.

Williams queried Jonathan on this point. If the
soldiers were wearing gray, they must have been Southerners, not Yankees.

"They ain't Southerners," Jonathan said firmly. But
the farmer was more concerned about the men who
were surrounding him than the color of their uniforms.
They wanted five sacks of potatoes, but they weren't
getting them for ten cents a bushel! The stubborn
farmer told the soldiers to keep their money.

Then George-Jonathan made terrible sounds of pain
and began to cough.

William spoke softly to him, tried to reassure him
that all was well, and let him speak again.

When the hypnotist had taken away the awful hurt,
Jonathan told him that he had been shot in the stomach
by the plundering soldiers because he would not take
their "damn money." The personality complained that
it still "hurt a little."

Williams progressed the farmer another five minutes

in the time of his last day of that incarnation. When he asked the personality what he felt at that point, Jonathan answered that he could feel nothing.

At the count of three, Williams brought the boy back to the present.

Williams was most eager to travel to Jefferson, North Carolina, to substantiate Jonathan's story and to attempt to confirm the physical existence of the personality from whom he had learned the apparent details of a previous earth life.

Due to the limitations of a close budget, Williams, his son Jack, and George Field decided to make a camping trip to Jefferson just as soon as school was out for the summer.

"Camping was a new experience for me," Williams wrote to me, "although both boys had had considerable experience with camporees in the Boy Scouts and had quite a bit of equipment. George had a tent that would sleep three, and between us we had plenty of sleeping bags. A friend provided camping stoves. Finally, much to my wife's dismay, a pile of equipment began to form on the dining room table, ready to be packed. Since we were traveling by Volkswagen, a careful list had to be made and every unnecessary item eliminated. We did consider it very necessary that we take my two tape recorders—the large one on which to play the tapes made in Keene (at the home of the president of the New Hampshire Psychic Research Society) and, if needed, to tape any conversations which we might have there where A.C. power was available, and a small portable for use in the car in and around Jefferson."

Williams was fortunate in that he had an old army buddy, who was now a minister serving a congregation in Watuga, Tennessee, living in Johnson City, just a short distance from Jefferson, North Carolina. The clergyman's backyard provided the expedition from New Hampshire with a base of operations from which to conduct its research in Jefferson.

Williams' enthusiasm and his hopes were high. He had visions of Jonathan-George running about recognizing familiar landmarks, leading them to his mother's grave, falling weeping upon his own burial place. Then it would be a simple matter to proceed to the courthouse and find all the records which would substantiate the previous existence of George Field in the physical person of Jonathan Powell.

"Things did not work out that way," Williams said.

Upon approaching the village, George claimed to have had strong feelings that he had been there before. Williams placed the teen-ager into a deep trance and regressed him to 1860. As he brought the boy's personality back to become Jonathan once again, he cautioned the lad to pay no attention to automobiles or other modern contrivances. Williams wished to take no chances on frightening Jonathan or to distract him with the puzzling artifacts of the twentieth century.

When Jonathan opened his eyes to Jefferson for the first time in over a hundred years, he was completely dismayed.

"Picture yourself, if you can," Williams wrote, "going back to your old neighborhood after a hundred years. There are all new houses and streets, and you are trying to find your own backyard."

When the investigators visited the Ashe County courthouse in Jefferson, they were disappointed to learn that the county had not recorded births and deaths before 1921! There had, however, been a registry of deeds.

On Page 430, Volume A, Williams and the boys found the copy of a deed in which a Stephen Reed had conveyed to a Mary Powell a parcel of land in 1803. This discovery excited the group very much. Jonathan had named a Mary Powell as his paternal grandmother. In 1803, Mary Powell would have been about the right age to be buying farmland. The investigators became even more sure of their research when they were told that Powell was a very uncommon name in that area.

The register of deeds referred Williams to a local historian who might be able to tell them the genealogy of the old families of Ashe County. Williams called the historian and made an appointment with her for that afternoon.

When the historian learned the purpose of Williams' expedition into North Carolina, she went firmly on record as saying that she did not believe in "this sort of thing."

She did, however, agree to offer what help she could. And, after listening to the tape recording of George-Jonathan's session at the Keene Psychical Research Society, she had to confess that she was most impressed with "Jonathan's" knowledge of Ashe County.

After the historian had heard the tape, Williams regressed George to Jonathan so that the woman might question the personality concerning the Ashe County of 1860.

"Remember to keep your questions in the present tense," Williams cautioned the historian. "To Jonathan it still is 1860!"

The historian queried Jonathan about a total of twenty-five persons and events in the history of Jefferson. Writing in *Fate*, Williams said that Jonathan knew nothing about some of them. He did, however, claim to know about fifteen of them, many in detail. He mentioned such things as these people's financial status, their children's names, and when they built their houses.

These details proved to be substantially correct. In the author's opinion he gave enough detailed answers to make any possibility of chance very remote.

In addition to the historian's confirming Jonathan's knowledge of the people and events of Jefferson circa 1860, she substantiated his claim that there had been a Mr. Brown who had served as a circuit-riding preacher. She could find no records of a Quaker church, but she rapidly conceded that a group might have met in private homes.

They replayed the tape which they had made when the historian questioned Jonathan about his life in Jefferson, Williams wrote. They wanted to once again get her reaction to his answers. To Williams, it seemed amazing and very significant that one who had never had any connection with Jefferson could know so much about it.

Williams recalled a humorous incident which occurred while he was riding about Jefferson with George and Jack. The boys asked him what the "snuff" was that they had seen for sale in numerous places in the village. In New Hampshire and in New England in general, the taking of snuff is practically a lost "art." Later that day, while shopping at a supermarket, Williams bought a can of snuff as a souvenir for each of the boys.

Williams had worked in the South and had seen the chewing tobacco used on many occasions. He explained to the boys what little he knew about the "taking" of snuff.

"About all I could really remember," Williams said, "is that the old-timers used to pack a wad behind the lip to get the flavor from it."

As the three of them were riding around the countryside a bit later, Williams regressed George to Jonathan. He hoped that Jonathan might recognize some landmarks and locate his farm, but then, suddenly, another idea occurred to the hypnotist.

"How do you like snuff, Jonathan?" he asked. "Do you want some?"

"I shore do!"

Jonathan had trouble getting the snuff out of "that kind of a box," but once he had the tobacco tin open, he set about "blowing" it in a skilled and expert manner.

Williams was startled. He had never seen anyone "sniff" the tobacco up the nose before. It took him a few puzzled moments before he remembered an article he had read which described this manner of using snuff as being the most popular method years ago. But it was still amazing to watch someone actually "sniffing" tobacco. It was an accomplishment which obviously took considerable practice and experience, not to mention a strong nose! Williams knew that George had never seen this done.

In his evaluation of the tape as compared with the uncovered evidence, Williams pointed out the difficulty of substantiating such a nondescript life as Jonathan Powell's one hundred years after his death. At the same time, the hypnotist stressed the fact that Jonathan-George spoke of an obscure village in a small North Carolina county, a place of which George Field would hardly be aware. "Jonathan" was able to identify and provide details of the lives of several old families of Ashe County. He was able to identify much of the country's typography which no maps of the area name. Then, too, there was a Mary Powell—a woman with an uncommon surname for the county—who bought farmland and who would have been the right age to be Jonathan's grandmother, just as the personality claimed.

Williams felt that one of the most significant parts

of the tape is Jonathan's description of his death. Jonathan claimed that he was shot to death by Yankee soldiers in gray uniforms because he refused to sell them potatoes. Even the most casual student of American history knows that the Yankees wore blue uniforms. Furthermore, Williams' research established the fact that there were no Northern troops in North Carolina in 1863.

"Once again, though," Williams said, "Jonathan was right. The local historian told me that at that time there were bands of renegades who came down from the north, using the war as an excuse to raid and plunder. They could well have been dressed in gray because they would have stolen their uniforms."

Shortly after the article appeared in *Fate,* Williams and George Field received further substantiation of Jonathan's existence in a letter from a woman who claimed to be the great-niece of Jonathan Powell. The woman went on to clear up a number of items which were unclearly stated by the personality of Jonathan.

"He [Jonathan] was killed by the Yankees, so my father said; but he didn't know any details at all about the case on how he was killed. Willard Powell was Jonathan's brother. Jim Powell was Jonathan's father [Jonathan stated that his father's name was Willard and that he could not remember having a brother]—and he was red-headed, or sandy haired; and all the family had blue eyes. We never knew what became of Willard or his family.

". . . My mother often talked about the Quakers and they would spend the night with her family over there. There was no Quaker church. . . .

". . . I haven't done any research on history, but a lot of those eastern Tennessee men fought for the South. That could have been some of them in the gray uniforms that killed Jonathan or it could have been the renegades."

In subsequent sessions of hypnotic regression, Williams led George Field back into three lives prior to his incarnation as Jonathan Powell.

"These were short lives in England in the fifteen- and sixteen-hundreds, so they are impossible to check," Williams told me. "They do, however, paint a vivid and seemingly accurate picture of life during those periods. In two cases, he was a girl, once a boy. In no case did he or she know his parents. It is a historic fact that during those years there were thousands of orphaned or deserted children living in the streets."

Although the transcripts of each of the lives is quite lengthy, Williams provided me with a capsule report of the three previous incarnations of George Field before he was born as Jonathan.

Number One. A girl. She has no memory of parents. She first remembers being cared for by a man who seems to be no relation. She lives in a one-room hovel and sleeps on a board. She is alone most of the time, and the man brings her just enough food to keep her alive. When she is about seven years old, the man dies. She takes to the streets, sleeping where she can, eating raw dough stolen from bakeries and whatever else can be found. When she is about twelve years old she is killed in the street by a horse and wagon. (A note of great interest here! This is the manner in which Jonathan said that his mother died. Could this mean something?)

Number Two. A girl. Her background and living conditions are similar to Number One. The most interesting thing about this experiment is that when taken through the death experience, she accounted all the symptoms of the Black Plague that swept England at the time.

Number Three. A boy. In this incarnation, he is again orphaned and deserted. [Jonathan could not remember his father, only that he had died at an early age. George Field lives with his widowed mother. Again, could a pattern be maintained in reincarnation?] As a twelve- or fourteen-year-old boy, he works around the docks and is on the sailing ships in port there. He seldom receives any pay, but he is given food for working. He enjoys most the work on the sails and the rigging.

The most amazing thing about this account, Williams related, is that when he regressed George Field to this life, he asked the sixteenth-century teen-ager if he could splice rope.

"I splice a lot of it," the personality told him.

Williams produced a piece on which the boy made a fast and expert splice. George Field has not even the faintest idea of how to go about splicing a rope. Rope splicing has become almost a lost art since the days of sailing vessels.

In life Number Three, George fell off the dock and drowned when he was about fifteen.

Loring G. Williams had numerous other cases in his files. At my request, he capsulized five major subjects whose claims of past lives were currently being investigated.

Subject Number One. In this present incarnation, Subject Number One is a woman of twenty-five. While under hypnosis, Williams has allowed her to recall two other lives.

Her first remembered incarnation took place in the United States about 1850, when she was born a boy who lived with his mother and sister in a cabin on a small farm. There was no father present, and the boy seems to feel that his sire has deserted them. When he is about ten years old, he leaves the cabin to go in search of his father. He realizes that the search is hopeless, but he does not return home. Instead, he becomes a drummer boy for the Union during the Civil War. After the war, he becomes a hermitlike creature who prefers to live alone in the woods for the rest of his long life. He acquires many animal friends in this strange, idyllic existence, but he becomes a misanthrope before he dies of old age.

In the woman's second remembered life, she is born a girl in England in 1678. Her parents die when she is about twelve, leaving only a small inheritance on which she might subsist. For two years she manages; then, at fourteen, she has spent all of her money. She is caught stealing and sent to jail. She spends a long time in jail and contracts tuberculosis before she is finally released on the condition that she sign a bond or indenture paper. The papers are sold to a ship captain who transports her to America for the purpose of selling the bond to someone in need of a servant (this was an old racket in those days).

By the time she has reached the colonies, she is weak, coughing a lot, and spitting up blood. She is sold to a plantation near Richmond where she works in the kitchen. She is the only white help there and she describes making many loaves of bread each day. She portrays the large brick oven in detail.

She enjoys life on the plantation much better than England, but her tuberculosis grows progressively worse. She dies at seventeen. She describes her funeral and watches herself being buried. She is glad that she died because she loves to float.

* * *

Subject Number Two. This volunteer for Williams' experiments is a boy who is presently sixteen years old. He has recalled two previous lives under hypnosis.

In his first life, he was born in Illinois about 1830–40. He has a small farm, a wife, and children. When the Civil War starts, he goes to Virginia and joins the Confederate Army. He experiences combat and is killed in action May 5, 1863, probably at the battle of Chancellorville. Williams has spent some time checking the records at Chancellorville, but of approximately 20,000 Confederate soldiers killed there, only a few hundred were ever identified.

The second life which Subject Number Two recalls carries him much farther back into time than the Battle of Chancellorville. He remembers being a black male slave who was born in ancient Egypt. He is forced to labor a fourteen-hour day with two meals per day as the architects of the Pharaoh construct a pyramid. Depressed at last with his hopeless life, he attacks a guard and is put to death at about the age of forty.

Subject Number Three. This thirty-five-year-old woman recalls one previous life. While under hypnotic control, she has regressed to the memory patterns of her life as a girl born in this country to parents of French extraction in the year 1790.

As a young girl, she is sent to France to become a governess for a rich family there. While working in this capacity, she meets a rich, old Frenchman and proceeds to marry him strictly for his money. After she has the man committed to the satisfying of her desires, she enjoys making his life, and the lives of his servants, just as miserable as she can.

The old man finally dies, much to her delight, leaving her the house, money, jewels, and servants. She becomes involved with a handsome young fortune hunter, who manages to relieve her of most of her money, but she still has her jewels. At last a maid, who has grown weary of her cruelty, kills her and steals her jewels.

Subject Number Four. This sixteen-year-old boy is able to remember owning a plantation and many slaves in the Kentucky of 1840. He recalls his wife and family. Most of all, he remembers the terrible Panic of 1857 when he is unable to sell his sorghum crop. By 1858, he has no money to feed his slaves. They revolt and kill him. After his death, he is able to watch over his family for about ten years, especially one son, who fought throughout the Civil War.

Subject Number Five. Williams' hypnotic prowess enabled this woman, who is now twenty-eight, to relive a past life as the daughter of a noble family in Poland in the early 1800's. True to the custom of the day, the subject remembers that her marriage was arranged for her by her family. She is pleased to discover that her young nobleman is handsome. In addition, he has a great estate, many serfs, and is governor of a territory. When she is about forty, she is thrown from her horse and killed. She has a huge funeral, which she is able to watch. She is also able to watch her family for several years after her death.

"Unfortunately the written word cannot convey the feeling that is expressed in the voice and actions of the subjects as they recount their past lives," Williams told me. "They sound old and weak as old age approaches; they register pain and distress when injured. If anything modern is brought to their attention, such as an electric light, a radio, or an automobile, they are amazed and usually frightened."

Williams pointed out that it is out of the question to check most of the cases. "In this sort of work, however, the fact that something cannot be proven does not make it false. In many cases the subject will recount accurate details of things that he could not possibly know.

"Under hypnosis and regressed to a previous life, many subjects possess skills that are normally quite foreign to them, and often are lost arts.

"If, in a former life, the subject was literate and could write, I will ask him to write something for me. When I compare the handwriting of the previous personality with the script of the present personality, I am able to see that the two styles are completely different. While regressed, the hypnotized subject is reliving another life in every detail.

"One argument that is often raised is that there exists a blood relationship between the person today and the prior incarnation. It is then claimed that the subject is just recounting old family stories that he has heard long ago but forgotten.

"I have never found any blood relationship from life to life.

"There is also the argument that the subject may be telling about someone or something that he has read.

"In the case of 'Jonathan,' the previous personality was from a small town, unlikely ever to have been heard of by George Field. Jonathan Powell was an obscure, poor, uneducated farmer, who would never make the history books, although he may now!

"Another argument which is often raised against the

reincarnation thesis is that the subject is only picking up a psychic record or image of one who has lived in the past and is not reliving his own past life.

"This can be accomplished through hypnosis, and I have done it. However, when this is done, the subject sees the people and events only as an observer, as if he were watching a movie. This is quite different from a regression to a subject's own previous life. When a subject is regressed, he relives the experiences which he describes.

"A phenomenon which can happen, and apparently does in some cases of spontaneous recall where the person has died recently and nearby, is the partial possession of a subject by a disincarnate spirit. This, of course, is considered to be nonsense by the materialists, but this belief was accepted by the early Christians. This is the reason cited for Jesus casting the demons into the herd of swine and then sending them on to drown."

I found correspondence with Loring G. Williams to be most fascinating and helpful. As for what his investigations prove, Williams said that perhaps each reader must decide for himself. The skeptic will proclaim that nothing has been proven, that there are no facts, only coincidences. The believer will proclaim that, at last, we have proof of reincarnation.

Williams tried to remain objective, but he could not resist the feeling that there was much more here than coincidence can account for. He believed that they found as much evidence for Jonathan as one could hope to find, after 100 years, of the life of someone who lived a short and unremarkable existence. He was convinced Jonathan Powell did live in Jefferson, N.C., from 1834 to 1863. After knowing Jonathan and visiting Jefferson with him, Wililams could believe nothing else.

CHAPTER FOUR:
SEEKING PROOF OF REINCARNATION

My correspondence with Loring G. Williams led to a friendship and a research relationship which lasted until his death in 1975. Together we investigated dozens of cases suggestive of reincarnation, and we taped hundreds of hours of men and women dramatically providing details of what seemed to be their past lives. Whether or not these reincarnational recalls prove the thesis of rebirth will, I imagine, depend largely upon the biases of the individual reader. Consider, though, the following:

When Williams returned with "Jonathan" to Jefferson village, their encounter with the historian yielded a great many veridical facts. For example, when the historian asked if Jonathan, placed in the time context of 1860, could remember Joshua Baker, the high sheriff of Ashe County, Jonathan gently corrected her by stating that Baker had been high sheriff ten years before, in 1850. Later, after brushing up on her knowledge of the old county records, the historian learned that this was true.

The historian asked about the drowning of Colonel George Bower, and she expressed some surprise when Jonathan seemed astonished to learn of the colonel's death. Again, after she checked her records, she found that Colonel Bower had drowned in 1864, four years later than the time sequence in which the regressed entity was transiently dwelling.

The guileless historian often phrased her questions in a manner that could easily have encouraged either conscious or unconscious lying or guessing on the part of the interviewee; but Jonathan answered the queries in a straightforward manner, regardless of the historian's promptings. When she insisted that he must have known the "rich old merchant Wall," Jonathan said that he did not, but that he knew Samuel Wall and gave the correct location of his home.

The historian, who was at first reluctant to participate in such an experiment, eventually entered wholeheartedly into the spirit of things, and she chuckled and nodded enthusiastically throughout Jonathan's vivid characterization of one of the wealthy members of Jefferson village society *circa* 1860. Later, when Jonathan indicated extensive familiarity with the historian's own ancestors, she seemed to be satisfied that she had not really embarked on a foolish chore.

In certain instances, Jonathan gave details of the ages, home locations, occupations, and marital status of Jefferson citizens. For those who would seize upon this assertion and attempt to convert it to proof of Jonathan's reincarnation being but a manifestation of "psi" ability (i.e., that he "picked" the knowledge of Jefferson's forebears from the historian's subconscious), one must immediately ask why Jonathan should apparently miss totally on the identification of other residents of that era. If George Field were but a brilliant clairvoyant and actor, why should he miss at all simply to make his performance seem more convincing? If one were out to hoax knowledge of a past life, the more perfect the score the better one would be able to deceive the gullible into accepting "proof" of reincarnation.

In going over transcripts of the sessions with the historian, Williams and I asked ourselves why it was that Jonathan seemed to know more of the obscure members of the village than he did the prominent, the wealthy, and the clergy. Part of the problem may have lain in semantics. When the historian asked if Jonathan "knew" such and such a prominent person, the poor dirt farmer may have taken the question literally. A hand-to-mouth farmer does not really "know" his banker, his attorney, or other wealthy professionals, even in a village as small as antebellum Jefferson. In a number of instances, Jonathan did, in fact, state that he "knew of" a certain individual. Perhaps this should have been picked up and clarified during the actual interrogation, and Jonathan should have been told that identification, rather than profession of intimate knowledge, was all that was being asked.

Then, too, Williams and I did not lose sight of the fact that the person of Jonathan Powell, as depicted through hypnotic regression, was basically a loner, who cared not at all for the society of women, little for the company of men, and who had abandoned churchgoing early in his life. Jonathan would have been the sort to have withdrawn from the leading citizens of Jefferson with whom the historian admonished him to get better acquainted.

Since the historian's interview of Jonathan Powell was much more than a yes-or-no quiz, it is impossible to provide the odds on his hits and misses. The historian asked Jonathan about a total of twenty-five persons or events in Jefferson *circa* 1860. The entity claiming to be Jonathan Powell readily admitted having no knowledge of some of them, but he did know something about fifteen of the individuals and items on which he was queried. Over fifty percent of his "hits" mentioned such correct details as financial status, physical descriptions, children's names, location of residences, and the construction of homes.

On one hand, it would be correct to say that George Field should have known *no* details about Jefferson "villie," North Carolina, in 1860. At the same time, he could have answered yes to every question. The fact that he offered correct details in his answers would seem to rule out the possibility of guessing. His misses only prove that Jonathan, the reclusive young farmer, did not know everyone in Jefferson. In our opinion, Jonathan gave enough detailed and correct responses to make the possibility of chance very remote.

"Nobody has as yet thought up a way that reincarnation could be proved in a laboratory test tube. But even in the laboratory we cannot escape from human testimony of some kind or other. In studying cases of reincarnation, I have to use the methods of the historian, lawyer, psychiatrist. I gather testimony from as many people as possible," Dr. Ian Stevenson, Chairman of the Department of Neurology and Psychiatry at the School of Medicine of the University of Virgina, told reporter Doug Laurie.

Dr. Stevenson has done more to put the study of reincarnation on a scientific basis than any other single individual. Certainly his academic and professional credits should convince even the most hostile skeptic that he is a man who would not be inclined to make rash judgments and crude assessments. Dr. Stevenson's "The Evidence for Survival from Claimed Memories of Former Incarnations" was the winning essay in the American Society of Psychical Research's 1960 contest in honor of William James, and his *Twenty Cases Suggestive of Reincarnation* was published by the ASPR in 1966.

In an analysis of the material with which he worked while compiling his winning essay, Dr. Stevenson discusses several hypotheses which he feels deserve consideration in attempting to comprehend data from cases suggestive of reincarnation. Among these hypotheses are the following:

Unconscious Fraud. Dr. Stevenson points out that in some cases other persons have attributed statements to the subject which he never made and in this way have permitted the initial story to grow out of proportion. The researcher terms this a kind of "collective hallucination" in which further statements are imaginatively attributed to the subject. Dr. Stevenson makes a very interesting point when he tells the reader that simply because so many of these cases suggestive of reincarnation have occurred in cultures where the populace accepts the doctrine of rebirth, one should not believe that the Hindus and Buddhists encourage their children to remember previous lives. On the contrary, he states, they consider it tragic if a child remembers a former existence, for this, they believe, presages an early death. Oriental parents often violently discourage their children from speaking of their alleged memories.

Derivation of the "Memories" Through Normal Means with Subsequent Forgetting of the Source. The researcher holds this hypothesis to be most often responsible for the many cases of psuedo-reincarnation. "We need to remember that we can acquire knowledge and subsequently forget our source of acquisition while recalling the facts learned," Dr. Stevenson points out.

He also quotes from the work of E. S. Zolik, who studied the ability of subjects to create fictitious former lives while under hypnosis. These fantasy personalities were the products of bits and pieces of characters in novels and movies and remembered childhood acquaintances because of the remarkable ability of the human mind to acquire paranormal information and to create fantasy personalities all its own. Dr. Stevenson cites yet another difficulty in serious research in cases suggestive of reincarnation: "We need to remember that items normally acquired can become mingled with those paranormally derived in the productions of persons apparently remembering past lives."

Racial Memory. Dr. Stevenson, a medical doctor as well as a psychiatrist, is well aware that man has not yet discovered the limits of genetic transmission. He feels, however, that such a theory applied to the alleged memories of previous lives which have survived investigation will encounter serious obstacles. He concedes that the hypothesis might apply in instances where it can be shown that the percipient of the memories belongs to a line descending from the personality whom he claims to be. But in most cases, the separation of time and place makes ". . . impossible any transmission of information from the first to the second person along genetic lines."

Extrasensory Perception of the Items of the Apparent Recollections in the Minds of Living Persons. Dr. Stevenson finds it difficult to accept the notion that an individual gifted with paranormal talents should limit the exercise of such abilities to communication with the specific living persons who have relevant items of information concerning the deceased personality from whom the subject claims to derive his memories. (Dr. Stevenson has usually limited himself to cases in which the percipient is a small child who is able to be transported among those people who knew the deceased personality in life. In cases in which the previous personality has been dead for a hundred years and all his friends, relatives, and associates have also passed away, the ESP hypothesis almost completely falls apart, except, as we have already noted, for such talents as psychometry making the clairvoyant seem a part of a scene of the past.)

Retrocognition. The researcher speaks of the question of this "psi" ability being responsible for cases suggestive of reincarnation by reminding us that the subject in such cases is always ". . . (a) at the scene of the retrocognized events, e.g., in Salisbury Cathedral; or (b) stimulated by some object connected with the events themselves or persons participating in them . . . ; or (c) in an altered state of consciousness, e.g., gazing at a crystal or in a trance." Such conditions do not, of course, apply to the great majority of cases in which an individual claims memories of a former existence.

Possession. Dr. Stevenson concedes that cases such as that of Lurancy Vennum seem to ". . . make plausible the hypothesis of temporary possession as an explanation for apparent memories of former incarnations." But in cases of possession, he tells the reader, the entity that has accomplished the transformation of personality usually does so solely for the purpose of communication with its loved ones on the physical plane and it never claims to be a former incarnation of the subject who has temporarily housed it. In true cases suggestive of reincarnation, there is no other personality claiming to occupy the body of the subject and the entity speaks of a former life, not of communication with surviving loved ones.

Dr. Stevenson believes that his accumulated evidence justifies ". . . a much more extensive and more sympathetic study of [reincarnation] than it has hitherto received in the West. Further investigation of apparent memories of former incarnations may well establish reincarnation as the most probable explanation of these experiences." Dr. Stevenson points out that in attempting to prove survival by evaluating mediumistic communications ". . . we have the problem of proving that someone clearly dead still lives." In shifting the emphasis of research toward an investigation of apparent memories of previous incarnations ". . . the problem consists in judging whether someone clearly living once died. This may prove to be the easier task and, if pursued with sufficient zeal and success, may contribute decisively to the question of survival."

We must not overlook the work of the Association for Research and Enlightenment, which, under the directorship of Hugh Lynn Cayce, has carried on the work of the celebrated Edgar Cayce. The work of Edgar Cayce is too well known to require elaboration in this book, but any researcher who has approached this work with an orthodox, but open, mind receives a powerful shock of recognition when he reads how the deeply religious seer of Virginia Beach felt upon hearing that he had spoken seriously and in depth of the doctrine of rebirth.

In *Edgar Cayce on Reincarnation,* author Noel Langley writes that when Cayce, "the most devout and orthodox of Protestants, a man who had read the Bible once for each of his forty-six years," heard his secretary read a transcript of the session he had just completed with a gentleman named Arthur Lammers, he was both frightened and bewildered. In trance, Cayce had stated ". . . flatly and emphatically that, far from being a half-baked myth, the law of reincarnation was a cold, hard fact."

Cayce's first fear, Langley tells us, was that ". . . his subconscious faculties had suddenly been commandeered by the forces of evil, making him their unwitting tool; and he had always vowed that if ever his clairvoyant powers were to play him false, he would permit no further use of them."

From 1925 through 1944 Edgar Cayce gave 2,500 readings which dealt with the Karmic patterns that had arisen out of the previous existences of those individuals who had sought out the seer's psychic assistance. To read even a part of the records of those readings is to be continually amazed at the enormous amount of substantiative information and details which were discovered in a great many of the cases.

A rather successful technique in the therapy of some kinds of mental illness is psychodrama, those spontaneous impersonations of the patient's problem in which he is given an opportunity to enact the conflicts which have inflamed his psyche. I have wondered if some of the cases suggestive of reincarnation might not be a kind of psychic psychodrama in which some segment of the subconscious seizes control of the subject during his regression and impersonates a fictitious personality for the purpose of providing insight into the darker recesses of the subject's character.

In cases in which an individual has made an accurate prediction of his contracting a particular disease, I have often felt that perhaps some transcendent level of his mind might have been subconsciously aware of the inroads of the disease upon the body quite some time before the overt symptoms of the illness began to manifest themselves. Perhaps during the individual's sleeping hours, when the conscious relaxes its control, the image of the disease may have been reproduced in the subject's dreams, thereby allowing him to "predict" the approach of the disease.

Could we have something of this sort in certain cases in which our regressed subjects recount what appear to have been other lives? Hypnosis frees the subconscious by simulating a sleeplike state which virtually anesthetizes the conscious mind. Perhaps regression permits a transcendent level of mind to dramatize some conflict of character, some weakness of moral fiber, or some approaching crisis by personifying itself as a previous physical embodiment of the present entity.

The fact that the regression personality is so often of a sex different from that of the entranced subject brings to mind Dr. C. G. Jung's theory of the *anima,* the female element in the male unconscious, and the *animus,* the male element in the female unconscious. In *Man and His Symbols,* M. L. von Franz, a pupil of Jung, writes: ". . . whenever one of these personifications of the unconscious takes possession of our mind, it seems as if we ourselves are having such thoughts and feelings. The ego identifies with them to the point where it is unable to detach them and see them for what they are. One is really 'possessed' by a figure from the unconscious."

If it is not some element of the subject's own unconscious playing the role of a previous incarnation, then perhaps in certain cases suggestive of reincarnation a discarnate entity has invaded the psyche of the living, eager to tell its story to the hypnotist. Dr. Carl A. Wickland's *Thirty Years Among the Dead* recounts many such possessions and has, since its publication in 1924, become one of the classics in the literature of the paranormal.

There are many documented cases of apparent spirit possession, including many which have occurred in contemporary times. Whenever I would propose possession as an alternative to reincarnation, Bill Williams would only shrug, admit the possibility, then add that he would have to discount it as a factor in any cases which he had personally investigated. "I have yet to see any evidence of spirit possession," he would tell me.

All that changed when a young sergeant, who had just been invalided home from Vietnam with several wounds, came to Bill with a story that he was being possessed by the spirit of a younger brother. Just a few months before, the sergeant, Ed, had been called home to attend the funeral of his fourteen-year-old brother, Marty, who was killed in a gun accident. Marty, who had stood six feet tall at the age of thirteen, was noted for his phenomenal physical strength. At the funeral, Ed said that he had felt the presence of Marty and had seemed to hear a whispered promise that Marty would "look after him."

After Marty's funeral, Ed returned to Vietnam where he was immediately involved in a serious battle. He was wounded, and blacked out. The young soldier may have been separated from his buddies and left for dead, but at this point Marty entered the body of the unconscious Ed and took control. With a speed and a strength which Ed had never possessed, and despite having been wounded in three places, he got himself to a hospital. Doctors were amazed when the severely wounded sergeant walked into the base. Ed remembers nothing after he blacked out from sustaining the wounds.

Now, the sergeant told Williams, it was apparent that Marty had saved his life, but it was also alarmingly apparent that Marty had liked the feel of a physical body once again. Ed had been conscious of Marty's constant presence and his repeated efforts to get into his body. Even as he sat talking to the hypnotist, the sergeant said, he could feel Marty's approach, which always was evidenced by a feeling of chill, prickly sensations, and goose pimples on his skin.

Bill brought Ed to the home of Professor Charles Hapgood, a man of varied experience who had dealt with cases of a similar nature in the past. In the Hapgood home, Bill placed Ed into trance. As soon as the young man was in deep trance, Marty took advantage of the situation to speak through his brother's vocal equipment.

The entity insisted that he only wished to protect Ed. Hapgood asked him if he did not realize how much his possessing Ed's body upset his brother. Marty said that he was unaware of making Ed feel uncomfortable and that he would continue to possess his body whenever he felt like it.

When Ed heard the tapes of Marty speaking through his mouth, he told Williams and Hapgood that he felt Marty wanted a test of strength. Marty had always been able to best his older brother in any contest of physical strength, but Ed felt that he now had the muscle power to win. He asked that Marty be allowed to take full possession for the contest. Williams and Hapgood counseled against such a test. Marty might not be so easy to pry out once he had taken full possession of a physical body. Ed continued to argue that Marty could only be bested in a physical contest.

"No sooner had Bill and I agreed to the experiment than Marty took over Ed's body right before our eyes," Professor Hapgood said. "There was a complete change in the control of the body's action and in the facial expressions. The body now acted physically like the body of a fourteen-year-old boy. The features were contorted into the expressions of a rather petulant, frustrated child. The body stood up and tried to grasp and raise the heavy chair in front of it by one leg. It did a very poor job. It seated itself again and there was evidence of great agitation. . . . Marty said the test had been unfair, because Ed had been trying to push him out. He wanted another try. Reluctantly, Bill and I assented to this. First, however, we had Ed try to lift the chair, which he did without any trouble, holding it steadily above his head with one hand. (He was then not in trance, and he explained that Marty had previously been able to beat him in such a contest of strength.)

"We assented to the second test. . . . Marty took over Ed's body with grimacings and contortions that reminded Bill of nothing less than Dr. Jekyll and Mr. Hyde. He then arose from his chair and bent to pick up the other chair, but could scarcely get it off the ground. After violent efforts, he tried his other hand, but he couldn't do it."

Marty admitted to Bill that he had been bested in a fair test.

"What are you doing to do now?" Bill asked the entity.

"I'm leaving," Marty said quietly. "I won't try to enter Ed's body again. But I'll come back again if ever he should need me."

Certain readers who have had a smattering of psychology in their academic careers will at once begin to theorize and conclude that the Marty-Ed case was just a rather dramatic case study in psychopathological phenomena. If one should study the literature of alleged "demon" and "spirit" possession, however, I think he would come to consider that there is something, perhaps as yet undefinable, but *something* more to such cases than neuroses running rampant.

Delusions of Memory. We are all well aware that our recollections of certain facts and experiences may become either dimmed or distorted through the passage of time. Such errors and illusions of memory are quite familiar to all of us and nearly all of us have lost bets and arguments when our memory of a particular happening has been demonstrated to be incorrect. We shrug off such minor embarrassments. After all, no one has a perfect memory.

When, however, some people recall what would seem to be a memory of a previous existence, they compound their error by adding interpretation to their faulty reproduction of a pseudo-memory. Let us illustrate by a hypothetical situation. We'll say that we are sitting around the fireplace some wintry evening discussing the fierce blizzard of '43. Suddenly our young friend, a schoolteacher in his early thirties, speaks up.

Yes, he says, he recalls the blizzard well. He remembers how the drifts were piled across the highways and how stranded motorists met grim deaths in the snow. His recollection of nights without electricity because of downed power lines is vivid. He even sings a few lines from the songs that were popular that winter. We are puzzled for a few moments, then express our amazement that our friend is so old. Of course, he was quite young, he assures us, but he remembers it all very well. We ask precisely when he was born. August 25, 1944. A strange look crosses his face, and we need say no more. How could he remember so clearly an incident which took place before he was born?

There is no mystery here. As a young boy, very often he must have heard his relatives discuss the big blizzard of '43. Perhaps every Christmas when his parents took him with them to visit his grandparents, there were whole evenings of reminiscences about the depth of the snow, how Uncle Mert, the salesman, got stranded and barely made it to the farmhouse, how the children made tunnels in the huge drifts. Our young friend may have been sitting on the floor playing with his new Christmas toys, but yet he was hearing it all; and the grim but exciting tales were making indelible impressions on his subconscious. It would be natural for the young man to make the transition from listener to participant and subconsciously claim the memories for his own.

James H. Hyslop dealt with such delusions of memory in 1906 in his *Borderlands of Psychical Research*. Hyslop observed that our conscious memories seldom extend back beyond the age of four. "When they do they usually represent some isolated or striking event that impressed itself on our minds. Usually, however, the life of that early period is forgotten. . . . Now if at any time some event should occur which recalled enough of the experience previous to that which represents our present consciousness of personality to make us feel that it belonged to a time previous, and yet we could not recall any sense of personality corresponding to it, we might be excused for describing the facts as representing a previous existence. It would be a perfectly natural illusion."

Delusions of memory may certainly explain many of the common "I've been here before" sensations which nearly everyone experiences from time to time. Delusions of memory may even explain certain instances in which a subject claims to remember a life immediately preceding his present existence.

I am convinced that possession—mental, spirit, "demon"—does occur, but in no case of possession with which I am familiar does the entity claim to represent a former life of the subject whose physical frame it has inhabited. The possessing entity is an invader (and usually makes no bones about it), not a reactivated memory pattern.

Because of my many years investigating "psi" (ESP) abilities of the human mind, it is very hard for me to let go of clairvoyance, telepathy, and psychometry as being the principal contributors to many cases suggestive of reincarnation. And because I think the creative potential of the human psyche is virtually unlimited, I find that a good number of cases could also be left at the doorstep of psychic psychodrama.

But there are always those stubborn cases that resist any theory other than the heretical, unspeakable doctrine of reincarnation. If clairvoyance provided George Field, the New Hampshire schoolboy, with information about the life of Jonathan Powell, a man who had died more than one hundred years before in a faraway Southern village, then young George's "psi" abilities must be developed to a degree which would enable him to pick up messages from a distant locale and concerning a man long dead. In order for a telepathic percipient to receive impressions, some living agent has to be "broadcasting." This means that a great many villagers in Jefferson, North Carolina, must have had Jonathan Powell on their minds at all times and were constantly "transmitting" psychic impressions of his life and colorful times. As we know, Jonathan Powell lived and died in obscurity. When Williams investigated in Jefferson, there was no one who had ever heard of the young farmer who had been shot in the marketplace by the "Yankees."

Once George Field had been brought to Jefferson, one might make some kind of case for the "psi" hypothesis, but it would be a very weak one. Why should George have singled out the farmer Jonathan for the object of his clairvoyance? Could Jonathan's murder have so supercharged the psychic ether in Jefferson that the impressions of this single act of atrocity reached out and touched a psychically sensitive teen-ager over one hundred years later? But if this were true, the impressions must have reached all the way to New Hampshire, and we have endowed George Field with superhuman powers of mind.

Clearly, in the case of Jonathan Powell and a good many of the other cases detailed in this book, there is more at work than ESP, genetic memory, spirit possession, psychic psychodrama, and delusions of memory. Can we, as products of twentieth-century Western culture, admit that reincarnation might well be that something more?

CHAPTER FIVE:
VIEWING DEATH AS TRANSITION, RATHER THAN TERMINATION

George S. Arundale in his *Nirvana* wrote: "There is no death, only change, and always change with a purpose, change to a greater end. Death is re-creation, renewal, the dropping of fetters, the casting aside of a vehicle which has ceased to suffice. Death is, in very truth, a birth into a fuller and larger life, or a dipping down into matter under the law of readjustment. Progress always, and progress toward Unity. We come ever nearer to each other and to the Real through death."

If a study of reincarnation begins to convince us that there is no death, only change, then we must next ask ourselves what part of the divine plan is served by placing each individual human soul on a cycle of rebirth.

J. G. von Herder *(Dialogues on Metempsychosis)* regards reincarnation as the same law of economy which rules through nature. The soul that has not become ripe in one life is put into the experience of living again until it has become perfected.

In flesh life, Herder remarks, ". . . the soul lies captive in its dungeon, bound as with a sevenfold chain, and only through a strong grating, and only through a pair of light and air-holes can it breathe and see. . . ." But it is through such repeated lifetimes on Earth that God trains us for ". . . a complete divorce from the sense-life."

It would seem appropriate at this point in our examination of reincarnation to present selections from actual transcripts of regressed hypnotic subjects reliving their alleged death experiences from past lives and, in some cases, their trauma of rebirth into life on the Earth plane of existence. These samplings have been gleaned from investigations which Loring G. Williams and I conducted from 1967 to 1972.

From a subject who has described a life in early Colonial America:

Williams: We'll count to three, and it will be five years later. You will tell me what's going on. One, two, three. Now what do you see?

Nothing. [The death experience has taken place.]

What are you doing?

Floating.

All right, I'll count to three again, and we'll go back to your last day as Abigail. One, two, three. Now what do you see?

(Violent spasms of coughing)

Abigail, you don't have to cough. I'll count to three and your coughing will stop. One, two, three. All right, you don't have to cough; you can tell us what's going on.

I'm sick.

Where are you?

The workhouse.

How old are you now?

I must be about seventeen. Yeah, I'm seventeen.

How do you feel? How has the cough of yours been?

Awful! It gets worse.

Do you still spit up blood now and then?

Oh, yes, all the time. Yes.

They don't do anything for it? There's nothing you can do?

No.

We'll go along and you can tell us what happens now. One, two, three. Tell me what's happening now.

I'm awful sick. I keep coughing and coughing, and I keep spitting up blood. I'm dying, and people tell me I'm dying.

Are you glad you're dying?

No. I don't want to die! I don't want to die! (Becoming hysterical) *No, I'm too young to die! I don't want to die, no! I can't die! I'm too young! I don't want to die! I'm too young to die!*

I'll count to three and it will be all over with. One, two, three. Now what do you see?

Nothing. [The tone of the voice is now relaxed, almost to the point of total indifference.]

Where are you?

Floating.

Can you see your body there?

Yes.

What's happened to it?

Nothing. It's lying there.

Is anybody attending to it?

Yes. The black mammy.

What's she doing?

She's cleaning me up, Oh, yeah.

Oh, now what's she doing?

She's lifting me into a pretty dress.

Now what's going on?

People are walking by.

Do they have you in a box or anything?

A pine one.

Do they have a preacher or anyone for you?
Yeah.
What's he have to say?
He just says I'm nice. Yeah, I was a good girl.
What do they say at the grave?
They just say from ashes to ashes, from dust to dust. Then they throw me in the grave. They cover me over.
What are you doing, just floating and watching all of this?
Yeah.
It doesn't bother you to watch?
Naw.
It doesn't hurt a bit, does it?
Naw.
Are you glad now that you died?
Yeah, I like it! I like to float!

From the regression of an entity who claimed a past-life as a latter-day "mountain man" in the Rocky Mountain region of Montana:

Williams: We'll let a few more minutes go by and you tell me what you see.
Somebody down there looks just like me.
Is it your body on the bed?
It looks like me.
Where's Tom?
Crying like the devil.
Is the doctor still there? What's he doing?
Just settin' in the chair, shaking his head.
Let time go on a little farther. You keep watching that body and tell us what they do with it.
Somebody pulled the blankets up over my face.
How do you feel now?
Comfortable and good.

Now what are they doing to you?

They picked it up. [His body has now become "it," as his detachment toward his fleshy environment continues to grow.]

Who?

Tom and that doctor.

Now what are they doing?

They're putting it out in the shack.

Is it winter?

Yeah.

What are they doing now?

They came back in the room.

Is your body still in the shed?

Yeah. [This was a common practice in the last century. When the soil of winter became too hard to spade, burial had to wait until spring.]

Let's go on to the next day. Tell me what they do with that body out in the shed.

They didn't do a thing to me.

Where's Tom?

He's building some kind of box. A long thing, with boards across the end.

We'll just watch him, and we'll see what he's doing as time goes on. Now what are they doing with the box?

They're . . . they're picking me up. They're carrying me.

Where are you, above somewhere watching?

Yeah, settin' up there somewhere.

Who's around there now?

Tom, his wife, that doctor, a man all dressed up in a suit. A preacher, I guess.

What are they doing?

The preacher is saying something.

What's he saying?

He's just talking how good I use' to be; how kind I was to the boys and everything. Now they're going to put their heads down and just look at the box. Tom and the doctor pick it up. They're going up through the woods with it. The doctor fell down.

Did he get hurt?

No, he got back up. They're going to a cave. Tom is shoveling away the snow. They pick up the box again, and they're going down with it. They just set the box on the floor.

Move ahead in time. Do you still see the box in the cave?

They caved the cave in.

They left the box in the cave? They didn't bother to dig a grave or anything?

No.

How long have you been watching, just floating?

Oh, I don't know. Been quite a while, I guess.

What year do you think this is?

Well, I don't know. It must be close to the turn of the century, I guess.

Do you see what's going on in the world?

I don't look down there much anymore.

You're very comfortable?

Yeah.

The death experiences of Jonathan Powell in Jefferson "villie":

Williams: I will count to three again, and it will be your last day as Jonathan. One . . . two . . . three. What are you doing?

I'm loading the sacks of potatoes . . . for those damn Yankee soldiers.

Are they coming to buy some?

Buy some! It's more like stealing them.
Why? Don't they pay you much?
No, I guess they don't. Here they come!
How many sacks of potatoes do they want?
Five sacks, and they ain't getting them.
Why?
They pay ten cents! I don't want your money! Ten cents for my potatoes! OH! (Sounds of pain and coughing)

It's all right now. I will count to three and the pain will be gone. One—two—three.
What happened?
They shot me. (Crying)
Where did they hit you?
In the stomach. (Gasping and sobbing)
Does it hurt now?
A little.
Why did they shoot you?
I wouldn't take their damn money.
How do you feel now?
It still hurts a little.

Time will go on about five minutes on a count of three. One—two—three. Now what do you feel?
Nothing. I can't see anything. I can't feel anything.
On the count of three you will come back to the present time. One . . . two . . . three.

In this instance, we spent some time permitting the entity to describe the period in between incarnations:

Williams: I'm going to count to three and it will be ten years later. One, two, three. Now what do you see?
Nothing. I don't see nothing. It feels darn good.
But you don't see anything?
I just see an old stone over there.

What does it say on the stone, or can't you read it?

It's got moss over it; it's old.

Are you dead?

I guess so.

How long have you been dead?

About eight years. Nine years.

Do you enjoy that?

Well, I don't know. I can't feel nothing, how can I enjoy it?

Do you ever see anyone by that stone?

Oh, yes.

Whom do you see?

Mrs. Jones' daughter once in a while brings flowers. She's getting old, boy.

Did you ever try to talk to her?

No.

Why not?

'Cause I don't want to, I guess.

How does time pass here? Does it seem that time is going on?

It feels all right to float up and down.

Do you enjoy it?

Yeah!

Now I'm going to count to three and we will go back again to your last day in this life. One, two, three. Now what's happening?

I just don't feel so hot.

Why?

I ache all over.

How old are you?

I must be close to thirty.

Now what's happening? Time is moving on a little bit.

The sheriff comes in. He brings me food. He looks at me and then runs out. Then this guy with the black suit comes in. There's two guys. One comes in, puts this thing on my stomach and it hurts. He has glasses on, and he shakes his head no. Then this other fellow, the minister of the peace or whatever you call him, he blesses himself or something.

Did they talk to you at all?

No, they didn't talk to me, they talked about me.

What do they do to you?

Well, a lot of townpeople come around the house and say, "Oh, what happened?" Some say that I was a good rider.

What do they do with you?

They're taking me over to this place to fix me up.

How do they fix you up?

I don't really know. I guess they're doing something to me. Cleaning me up and stuff.

Now what are they going to do?

Now they're putting some stuff on my face. I guess he's painting it a reddish color. Then he puts me into this suit, I guess. He puts this floppy thing down my shirt. He looks like he's choking me with it.

Can you feel it?

No.

Now what are they doing?

Now they're putting me in this wooden box. It's a funny shape. They shut it, put nails around it. People come after that and put flowers around it.

What did they do with the box then?

The next day they picked it up, about six guys, and they first put it in a carriage. Then they start walkin' with a bunch of people behind them. Some folks wore black, and the women were crying like babies and stuff. They got me up to the old cemetery, was up past where I use' to live. They had to walk umteen miles.

Is Mrs. Jones' daughter there?

Yes. She's just crying. They got me up there, these two old guys, I guess, that got done digging a hole. I didn't know what they wanted the hole for, but after a while I found out. They put a guy in it. Put me in it, I guess it was! They said a bunch of words.

Does it bother you to watch?

No. Why would it bother me? I don't feel anything.

Then what happens?

After that some folks start walking away. Mrs. Jones' daughter just sat there by the minister and she bawled her head off. One brought a little box for that water in that little hole. Now they're covering me up with dirt.

Do you watch them now?

No.

What do you watch?

I don't know. I'm just going up in the clouds, I guess. I watch different people. I see people dying and watch people crying.

Did you see Mrs. Jones' daughter after she died?

Oh, yes.

Did you get a chance to talk to her?

No.

Why not?

I didn't want to.

Does she want to talk to you?

I guess so. I don't want to talk to her.

You just watch people?

Yes.

Time goes on and then all of a sudden you're born again, aren't you?

I don't see that.

Let's go back six months to a year before birth. Tell me what you're doing and what you see?

I don't see nothing: I'm sleeping.

What made you decide to be born again? Did you have anything to say about that?

No, sir! I guess not.

I'll count to three and we'll go back to six months before you were born. One, two, three. Now what do you see?

Nothing.

How do you feel?

Cooped up or something. [Is he describing the sensation of being confined to the womb?]

Let's go back another three months. One, two, three. Now what do you see?

Nothing. [Does the soul enter the body at six months? The subject felt "cooped up" at six months, but feels nothing at what would correspond to the first month of pregnancy.]

Still looking around?

Oh, yeah, still up in the clouds. Boy, I see this funny thing going around. [At what would be the first month of his mother's pregnancy, the subject claims to be floating, "still up in the clouds."]

Do you ever think about coming back to earth?

I like it right where I am!

In our research, Loring Williams and I found an average of what appeared to be approximately eighty years between lives. We were by no means dogmatic about this finding, because we occasionally found instances in which only a few decades, or even months, had passed before incarnations. In this case, Williams carefully led the entity up to birth in its present life experience:

Williams: Are you still floating?

Yeah, I'm just floating.

You're going to float on a little more, a little more, nearer today now. What do you see?

Just things. I don't know. People. There's a field near a beach. There's lots of people.

What's your name?

I don't know. I don't have a name.

Are you still floating?

No, I'm there! I'm watching!

What are the people doing?

I don't know! (Becoming excited) *I don't know what they're doing, but they're awful. They're hurting him! It's awful! They're awful.* (Beginning to cry) *They're hurting him!*

We'll go on to three years later. One, two, three! Now what do you see?

I see a house.

Where?

I don't know. It's just a little house. It's cute.

What's your name?

Mar-r-y. (Drawing out the name in little-girl fashion)

How old are you?

Two!

We're going back to your first day as Mary. You can tell me all about that. One, two, three. Now what do you see?

Black.

I see. What are you doing?

Nothing.

Where are you?

I don't know.

All you see is black?

Yep.

In just a few minutes now you will have to see something. One, two, three. Now what do you see?

White.

Where are you?

I don't know. Oh, look at the people! Oh!

What are they doing?

I don't know. Oh, a lady there!

What's she doing?

I don't know!

What's she got on?

White.

What do you have on?

Nothing.

How big are you?

I'm little. Yeah, real little! Awful little!

What's your name?

Mar-r-y.

How old are you?

I'm about two minutes old!

Do you remember being born?

Nope. All those people are happy. Ha-ha! Ha-ha! (Begins to laugh wildly)

I'll count to three now, and it will be the next day. One, two, three. It's the next day. What do you have on today?

A pink nightie.

Do you like that? Is it comfortable?

Yeah, I like it. (Then, changing her mind) *My hands are tied in, though: I don't like that. I don't like my hands tied. It's awful.*

I'm going to count to three, and it will be six months later. One, two, three. Now what do you see?

I'm with my daddy. I've never seen him before. He's my daddy, though. [Mary's father had been in military service at the time of her birth and was unable to see his child until she was six months old.]

What are you doing?

I'm on my daddy's lap, and they're taking pictures of me.

Is that fun?

No, I don't like that. I cry.

What do you have on? Are you all dressed up for the pictures?

I've got a pretty white dress on. Yeah, it's got green, white, and red things on it. It has white and green things down like this, and great big green buttons, and white and green things around it like this. It's cute. I like it. My hair is curly.

Do the excerpts from the various case studies recounted in this chapter clarify the concept that death is a transitional state, rather than a termination of existence? Just as each individual, in the final analysis, faces the death experience alone, so must each reader interpret the import of these cases to fit his own particular concept of the true nature of death.

It was in his *Parerga and Paralipomena* that Schopenhauer made his oft-quoted remarks concerning reincarnation: "The individuality disappears at death, but we lose nothing thereby; for it is only the manifestation of quite a different Being—a Being ignorant of time, and consequently, knowing neither life nor death. The loss of intellect is the Lethe but for which the Will would remember the various manifestations it has caused. When we die, we throw off our individuality, like a worn-out garment, and rejoice because we are about to receive a new and better one."

CHAPTER SIX:
DICK SUTPHEN'S GROUP REGRESSION TECHNIQUES: PAST LIVES EN MASSE

He is a tall, slender man with a pleasant manner and a soft voice. He is a skilled and masterful hypnotist, who appears as the very antithesis of the popular stereotype of a mind manipulator.

Dick Sutphen looks as though he had come prepared to ramrod a herd of cattle to Abilene rather than to guide men and women back to what may be significant former lifetimes. Faded jeans, open-necked cowboy shirts, scuffed boots, a wide-buckled belt, and a friendly grin do not appear to make a Mandrake of the mind; but, as one learns so often in life, appearances can certainly be deceiving. Watching Sutphen at work with a roomful of people must rank as an impressive exercise in harnessing the elusive psyche.

The words that come from his mouth are well formed, well articulated, interestingly mixed with hip-jive expressions, the jargon of the metaphysical field, and an occasional allusion to classic psychoanalytic literature. The man, if not Renaissance, is unquestionably well rounded.

Fifteen years or so ago, we would have met him as an advertising agency art director, servicing major accounts. As a free-lance designer/illustrator, he has won hundreds of show awards for his creative efforts. He has produced twelve volumes for the professional art market, published five love-poetry titles, and authored the best-selling *You Were Born Again to Be Together*.

For the past ten years, Dick Sutphen has focused an intense involvement in the psychic-metaphysical world. His hypnosis work began in 1972, and he set about almost at once to develop a technique whereby he might hypnotically regress a roomful of people at one time.

"To the best of my knowledge," Dick told me, "no one had ever done group regression to alleged former lives before this time. Every hypnotist told me that there was no way to do it."

The first group regressions were conducted in the Sutphen home, in Phoenix-area colleges and high schools, and in metaphysical gatherings in the area. In 1973, Dick founded and directed a hypnosis/metaphysical center in Scottsdale, Arizona. The convenience of working at an established center provided him the structure he needed to experiment extensively with both individual and group techniques and the opportunity to amass a large number of case histories for purposes of comparison and contrast.

At the present time, Dick Sutphen is conducting seminars with his attractive wife Trenna, doing individual hypnosis work and research in Arizona, and writing metaphysical material.

"What reincarnation is, or is not, is really not the point," Dick Sutphen emphasized. "Past life regressions in themselves, unless used for a purpose, are no more than an amusement.

"I (and many others) have perfected hypnotic regression techniques to such a degree over the past few years that anyone can view their own past lives. I could give you hundreds of Bridey Murphys on a few days' notice.

"What is important, in my opinion, is: If reincarnation is valid, then what does it mean to me and to mankind? How can such knowledge of *reality* be related to the here and now?

"Hopefully the following capsulized versions of several real-life case histories will help to illustrate the positive possibilities of continued exploration and research."

CASE HISTORY/DENISE

Denise Walsh, a formal-looking, middle-aged woman, had attended several of our weekly metaphysical investigation sessions at our center in Scottsdale, Arizona. After an evening of group hypnotic regression, and a lecture on Karma, she asked if I'd talk to her privately for a few minutes.

"Would you make me an appointment for an individual regression session?" she asked. "I think there are some things I need to explore."

I explained that my secretary would be glad to schedule her if she'd call the following morning during office hours.

"Did something happen in the group session tonight that triggered this need?" I questioned.

"I only received flashes and quick inner visions of myself as a man, and I was screaming and yelling. Can you hear things in regression? I swear I heard myself stating an allegiance to Diocletian and cursing another group? Maybe it relates somehow to my present problems?"

"Sometimes a group regression is a good way for the subconscious to release something that is being repressed, or causing hidden anxieties," I explained.

"Have you ever heard of a Diocletian, or does it relate to anything in your present life?"

"No," she decided after a moment's thought, "but I was just fired from my job. I can't seem mentally to recoup from the shock. And I'm going to be in economic trouble very soon if I don't manage to get a hold of myself."

Prior to the first regression session, Denise explained how she had maintained a position of ever-increasing authority for twelve years within a large Phoenix-based insurance company. She admitted that she enjoyed "using her power," and was not well liked by other employees. As the result of an administrative shake-up, she was assigned to a new supervisor, who took an immediate dislike to her. A few weeks later she was fired.

Well after the hypnotic regression sessions I am about to describe were completed, I talked to someone else who had worked at the same company during Denise's tenure.

"She was an absolute tyrant," he explained. "Denise expected everyone in that office to do her bidding . . . including those above her. When she started her normal routines on her new boss, he just eliminated the problem by getting rid of her."

Two private sessions were conducted, and the following information was retrieved from previous centuries:

In the year 294 A.D., during the decline of the Roman Empire, Denise was a man named Carius. He resided in England as a provincial supervisor under Emperor Diocletian. His appointment had been made by a special governmental committee, and during a period of revolt by the English people, Carius found himself in the position of directing large numbers of Roman soldiers. He did not have a background as a military man, and a conflict soon developed with the Roman officer in charge.

Carius favored excessive cruelty and mass violence as the most effective means of regaining civil control. The officer advocated the use of restrictions and the limited use of violent examples to create an environment of hardship and fear, thus achieving the same end result.

In the end Carius negotiated the recall of the officer and his demotion. Under the new Roman officer assigned to the province, Carius' plans were instituted, but resulted in years of conflict and never-ending turmoil for all involved.

While she still was in deep hypnosis, I directed Denise up into the "Higher-Self" mental realms. This is a matter of using special techniques to allow the subject to tap in on the "all-knowing" mental levels of the superconscious mind—the ninety-five percent that we do not normally use. From this perspective she explained that she still had not learned to use power correctly. That until she does, she will be "toppled."

"It is so simple," she said. "I must simply be kind and loving toward all . . . those above and below me in an authority position. Then there is no limit to my ability to achieve."

She also explained that the Roman officer in the past life was the supervisor who fired her in the present life.

Karmic balance! Cause and effect! Denise told me that she was going to find another position, and she felt she'd never misuse authority again. I haven't heard from her, so I don't know what has transpired in the last five years. Hopefully, past-life hypnotic regression proved to be a positive tool for understanding, thus helping her to create a new and positive personal reality.

The historic facts of this case were all valid, although consciously Denise had never heard of Diocletian; and she had never studied the Roman Empire in any depth during her high school years.

CASE HISTORY: JORDAN AND MONICA CALLAHAN   Fall 1976

"Our request is probably the most simple, yet most totally impossible one you've received all week," Monica quipped. "We want to know why, after seven years of marriage, our relationship is falling apart?"

I couldn't help smiling at the couple sitting across the table from me in the Scottsdale restaurant. Both were in their mid-thirties and participants in a five-day, Past-Life Seminar I was conducting in Scottsdale, Arizona. It was the evening dinner break of the third day. Like most of those attending the seminar, Jordan and Monica had come from another state to take part in the activities.

"I'm glad your request isn't complicated," I laughed. "What can you tell me about the situation? Simplify it down to a few sentences if you can."

They looked at each other, hesitated; then Jordan spoke.

"I guess I have to admit that I feel threatened or something. Monica wants to get out into the world more. She wants the freedom to come and go as she pleases. I even got a knot in my stomach when I see her reading *Playgirl* and *Viva*. Maybe I worry about being inadequate? I just wish she were happy staying home with the kids, like she always has been in the past."

"What kind of relationship do you desire, Monica?" I asked.

"I'd just like to be free to be me," she replied with some underlying hostility in her voice. "I don't want a sexually open relationship, but I don't want to have to answer for every minute of my day, or get into a fight with Jordan because I have an innocent drink with a male friend. We used to have a fine sex life, but our constant hassles have caused it to go downhill for the last several months."

Jordan silently nodded in approval with her statements.

"Well, as you already know, I'm not a marriage counselor," I told them. "You've already heard my spiel about man/woman relationships from a metaphysical perspective."

"Yeah, that seemed to be supportive of Monica's present directions," Jordan replied.

"I don't think he'd have attended if he'd known that lecture was on the agenda," Monica stated, pointing her thumb at her husband.

"Now wait. This isn't a matter of taking sides," I said. "I do believe in a relationship of freedom and trust between two people, because I've seen it work better that way. But you are experiencing very real anxieties, Jordan. Possibly if you could fully understand them, you could begin to rise above them. We all think we have problems; yet it isn't the problem that concerns us. It is the effect of that problem. How we mentally let it affect us.

"Once you are no longer mentally affected by a problem, you no longer have it . . . although nothing external may have actually changed in your life.

"How have you been receiving in the group hypnotic regression sessions?" I asked, directing my question to Jordan.

"It was slow at first," he replied. "But the impressions have become much more vivid and real with each session we've done."

"I have to use my full energy on the seminar itself," I explained, "and since I've already conducted the individual demonstration sessions, there is no way for me to work with you individually before the seminar is over. But you're now conditioned. Why don't you work with John [a backup regressive hypnotist who often works in association with my seminars] in an individual session or two? I'll talk to him about the direction I'd like him to explore."

If I'd been conducting the session myself, I might have attempted what I call a "double past-life chakra-link" between Jordan and Monica, but this is complicated, difficult, and still in the experimental stages. When it works it is spectacular, for both people experience the same past life at the same time; and there is usually no question about the validity of the experience. In this situation I asked John to work first with Jordan, and if necessary include Monica in a second or third session.

As it turned out, Jordan's regression was all that was necessary for an understanding of his present anxieties about his wife.

Summary of the session: Jordan saw himself as a woman named Ena, working in a bakery shop in England in the mid-1700's. She eventually met and married a young man named Carlton (Monica), who made his living traveling through the country selling various tobaccos for a London importer.

On one occasion, after they had been married for

YOU WILL LIVE AGAIN 91

three months, he was badly beaten and robbed while away on business. Two months of convalescence were required before he could return to his work. A year later Ena was pregnant, and the marriage was happy. Yet Carlton did not return from a sales trip. They never saw each other again and his fate was never known.

"You're still afraid that if Carlton, who is Monica in this life, goes out into the world she'll be hurt, or you'll lose her," I explained to Jordan.

"I don't need to explain what is so obvious, but you must be aware of how effectively this past-life experience has programmed your subconscious mind. You can allow the anxiety from another life to ruin this life—or through this understanding you can release it and be done with it. If you don't, it will probably carry forward into your next life."

"Yeah," he smiled, slowly nodding his head in approval. "But do you think it's all right to ask her not to take up tobacco selling this time around?"

Trenna Sutphen works in many ways during the past-life seminars, but probably the most dramatic is her ability to perceive the past lives of others and then provide them with present-life psychic information from the Higher Self hypnotic levels.

For a Chakra Hook-Up demonstration in each seminar, a volunteer is chosen from the participants. Trenna now lies down on a bed on the stage while the subject sits behind her in a chair. Dick begins to hypnotize her and, as part of the induction, completes an elaborate set of instructions which connect the top three energy chakras of the two people.

A very real "psychic link" is now established, and Dick usually induces an even deeper trance.

When this is complete, he instructs Trenna to draw upon the connecting link and allow the memories from their subconscious mind to flow into her own. She is now instructed to begin to relive a portion of a past life that would be of value for the volunteer subject to know of in the present.

Los Angeles: The volunteer was a woman of approximately thirty. Trenna was speaking in the voice of a small child of seven or eight. She was listening to a big fight between her parents, and found out that her daddy was not her real father. Mother had been pregnant by someone else at the time of the marriage. After this the father left and never returned. When Trenna was moved out of the past and into the Higher Self, she explained many things about the present life and its relationship to other times.

Once Dick had awakened Trenna, he asked the volunteer if any of it made any sense.

"Everything she said . . . everything she said that I know about," she explained. "Plus, I've had a reoccurring nightmare all of my life. It's always the same. My father, in my present life, is not really my father. I've had it ever since I was a little girl and it has haunted me," she now started to cry.

"You won't ever have it again," Dick explained.

San Francisco: The volunteer was a woman of approximately thirty-five. Trenna was speaking in a fearful voice about hiding in the cellar with her eighteen-year-old sister. She was sixteen. Upstairs they could hear German soldiers searching the house.

The soldiers found the girls and started to carry the sister off to another room. The sixteen-year-old began to scream and wouldn't stop, which angered one of the men to the degree that he grabbed her and strangled her to death. Trenna also related much accurate contemporary information about the woman's life.

Even before awakening Trenna, the volunteer was shaking and crying, just listening to Trenna relate the situation.

When Dick asked her about it, she completely broke down.

"Oh, my God," she sobbed. "All of my life if anyone so much as even touches my neck I become hysterical and it takes me hours to calm down. I know that is what happened. . . . I could see it transpiring while she talked. Plus everything she said about my current life is absolutely accurate, even down to the young, black-haired boy in my life."

Dallas, Texas: The volunteer was a man of approximately forty. Trenna was telling of a sea captain lifetime, and an event that transpired in 1897. The captain had eliminated half of the necessary lifeboats to provide more cargo-carrying space. There was an explosion on board the ship, and when the ship started to sink he was the first to make a space for himself while half his men drowned. During the night he threw a wounded man out of the lifeboat to conserve water. Those who remained in the boat eventually threw him overboard.

From the Higher Self, Trenna explained that all of his present life he has had a paranoid fear of taking any form of responsibility, and that he continued to punish himself for something that happened in the past.

"You have constant deep depressions, and your stomach becomes a spasmodic knot on a regular basis," she said. "This all relates to this past life and it is time you let go of the guilt. Let go of it now. Use your time in this life to help others. Only you can erase this Karma, by believing you can."

"I believe she touched something, didn't she sir?" Dick said, looking at the now white-faced volunteer.

"Everything! Everything! Even down to the knot she talked about. I began to have the stomach spasms in the middle of the regression. Yes, I've spent my life hiding from any form of responsibility. Yes, the up-and-down depressions have bothered me all of my life." He buried his face in his hands, explaining that he couldn't talk about it for a while.

Trenna developed her unique abilities over the years of working together with her husband. She can even hold a letter from someone who is troubled and, with the same hypnotic techniques, form a long-distance link, through which she has accurately described the past lives and present-day effects. It must be mentioned that she is not available to do this sort of work privately or via the mail, under any circumstances, for it is a fantastic drain.

CASE HISTORY/BARBARA

In May 1977, my wife Trenna and I were conducting a Past-Life Seminar in Atlanta, Georgia, along with Brad Steiger, Francie, and Grant Gudmundson. Barbara was one of the participants, and she had traveled all the way from Houston, Texas, to attend.

"Why did you come this far for a two-day seminar?" I questioned.

"I missed you when you were in Houston, and something, or somebody, up there told me it was really important to experience this," she smiled back at me. "I have several problems. Some you can see, and some you can't."

She was obviously referring to her excessive weight —225 pounds—being carried by an attractive twenty-nine-year-old woman. I'd observed her earlier in the day during the first two group regressions, trying to be comfortable in two chairs because her weight made lying down on the floor impossible. As a deep-level somnambulistic subject, she practically fell off the chairs the moment I began the induction.

As part of the Saturday evening seminar demonstration sessions, I always do some individual regression work so everyone understands how the verbal questions and answers work. On this particular night, I asked Barbara if she'd like to participate. She agreed, along with eleven others. I gave them all the following instructions:

"I want you to think about something in your life that you want to change. It can be any kind of problem, habit, or personal situation. In a moment I'm going to hypnotize you; and when I touch each of you on the hand, I'll be talking directly to you and only to you. I will count backwards from three to one; and on the count of one, you are going to move back in time to the cause of your present problem—if indeed the cause lies in the past, in this life, or in any of your previous lives. You will see and relive this situation before your own inner eyes, and thus you will understand the problem and begin to release it."

Group hypnosis was now completed, and I began to move down the line, touching each subject on the hand, counting backwards from three to one, then saying, "Speak up now and tell me what you see and what you are doing!"

The subject's reaction is always a surprise and usually emotional, for he is being directed back to the cause of his problem, which, more often than not, is a traumatic situation. Many people who have watched the sessions I've conducted on national television shows have asked how I've achieved such emotional regressions so quickly. This technique explains it.

This night a man was carrying out in anguish as he relived an ancient battle.

A young woman was reliving a situation of being lost in the woods as a small child.

A middle-aged woman was starving to death in an African community.

And when I came to Barbara, she cried out, screamed, and began to shake. Her voice was that of a young girl, "Oh, no . . . no, no, no . . . oh, no please! Please! Why are you doing this to us?"

Her reaction was too extreme to allow her to continue under the present circumstances.

"Return," I commanded and her body went limp as she relaxed into a peaceful, hypnotic sleep.

After all of the subjects had been awakened, I asked Barbara if she'd like to explore in more detail the prior life she'd touched on. This time, I told her, it would be on a one-to-one basis, so that I could devote all of my attention to her. Once again, she anxiously agreed.

The hypnotic trance was induced again, and she was instructed to return to the same lifetime, but a month earlier. She was soon speaking in the voice of a twelve-year-old French girl, describing her luxurious home and life in eighteenth-century France at the time of the Revolution.

When moved forward in time, she experienced the arrival of soldiers to take her family to prison. Numerous humiliations followed, and she was eventually killed by the revolutionaries.

From the Higher Self, when asked how this French life related to today, Barbara cried out, "Pretty people get hurt! I was so pretty, and they killed me. The only way to be safe is to remain ugly to the world. Then you'll be safe . . . then you'll be safe!"

After awakening her, additional information was provided. Barbara explained how she'd gone to the best reducing organizations in Texas, but she could never lose weight. She would begin to lose, then she would panic and go on an eating binge to bring her right back to 225.

One well-known specialist told her, "Once you find out why you psychologically need to retain weight, you'll be able to let go of it."

"You know you can do that *now,* don't you, Barbara?" I asked.

"Oh yes, I know I can!" she beamed back.

"Past-life hypnotic regression can be used as an extremely valuable therapeutic tool to explore the cause of subconscious anxiety, repressed hostilities, hidden fears, hang-ups, and interpersonal relationship conflicts," Dick Sutphen explained. "It isn't a magic wand, and the past-life causes don't always surface as quickly as in the case histories I've described here. But it does work, and it can be for many the first step to letting go of a problem.

"Psychiatrists often spend months or even years searching for the cause of their patient's problem. They are aware that in understanding the cause they can begin to mitigate and, eventually, eliminate the effect. Yet by limiting their search to the time frame of one life, they may never find the origin of present conflict.

"Over the last year I've shared my own techniques

with several psychologists around the country, and they report that they are achieving equally effective results. Their patients are getting well. Wisdom erases Karma," Dick concluded.

CHAPTER SEVEN:
A NEW AGE VISIONARY
ANSWERS AN AGE-OLD QUESTION

I had been lecturing at a two-day seminar in up-state New York when a friend who lived in the area, knowing of my perpetual interest in interviewing men and women with remarkable or unusual abilities told me that I would have to talk to the "angel."

"I beg your pardon?" I asked, wondering how he would arrange such celestial communication.

He laughed at my momentary confusion, then added: "Her name is Francie, but she looks like an angel and she claims to talk to angels."

Way back in my youth during the currently fashionable fifties, I recalled Eddie Fisher plaintively asking in song how one might speak to an angel; but I found little difficulty in communicating with Francie when I met her quite by accident later that same day. Although she seemed very shy and was soft-spoken and unassuming, she did indeed seem to emanate an angelic radiance. When one combined this high vibratory aura with her long blond hair, warm brown eyes, and lovely smile, he could easily ascertain just how she had earned the nickname of Angel.

What of her claim to communicate with multidimensional beings?

My many years of research into several facets of the paranormal had convinced me that such contact with intelligences external to mankind was not only possible, but quite likely.

According to a recent Gallup Poll, three in ten respondents stated that they had experienced a moving religious experience and "other-worldly feelings of union with divine beings." And the respondents' sex, education, or age did not make a significant difference in their answers.

Dr. Elisabeth Kübler-Ross, the eminent doctor who has revolutionized our view of death and dying, told a hushed audience of several hundred psychologists, psychiatrists, and mental health experts attending a medical conference in San Diego that she had been visited the night before by three "spirit creatures" who had instructed her to tell the assembled doctors about the reality of the spirit world.

Dr. John Lilly, the pioneering neurophysicist, biologist, psychoanalyst, and distinguished explorer of inner space, related his encounters with his spirit guides in his famous work *The Center of the Cyclone*.

As Francie and I spoke over a large tossed salad at a nearby restaurant, I quickly learned that she is one of the sensitive persons who is somehow able to glimpse the "in-between universes" and who has maintained contact with multidimensional intelligences—or angels and guides—since she was a child. Although she had once been a teacher of Raja Yoga, I found that she chose at the present time to serve as a channel for teachings from her Parent-Guide.

"I believe that everyone has both a Parent-Guide entity and a Guardian Angel, Brad," Francie said. "The Parent-Guide sees that one's present lifetime affords the necessary learning. The Guardian Angel comforts and protects one throughout life's learning and trials."

Francie remarked that she was but a "facet of her

Soul," and that comment triggered my subconscious to think of a theory of reincarnation which had occurred to me after more than a decade of seriously researching the subject: Rather than each soul-personality reincarnating again and again to learn and to progress on the Earth plane, perhaps there may be a Soul-in-common for several materially manifesting personalities.

In other words, let us say that I seem to recall a life as a galley slave, *circa* 100 B.C.; a lifetime as a Viking, *circa* 1100 A.D.; an existence as a French diplomat, *circa* 1700; and a rugged time as a fur trapper, *circa* 1820. It may be that I, Brad Steiger, did not literally live those former lifetimes as the same personality being reborn, but that my present self-manifestation is able to tap into memories of growth and spiritual evolution which have been absorbed by a common Soul.

In this theory, the Soul may have materially expressed itself in hundreds of lifetimes and will have assimilated the growth memories acquired by each of those physical manifestations, but each of those personalities has lived but once. It may be that the particular lessons learned by the galley slave, the Viking, the diplomat, and the fur trapper are especially applicable to my present existence; but I was not actually any of those individuals in a previous life experience. I am only able to tune into certain storage cells of spiritual wisdom and knowledge in the common Soul in order to aid me in acquiring even more growth activity in my present Earth plane struggle.

I was excited to learn that Francie had received a vision teaching on "The True Meaning of Life," which was very harmonious with the concept which I had assumed, perhaps arrogantly, that I had developed strictly through my intellectual processes.

Although she related the entire vision to me at the

time in her own oral tradition, the vision has since been expressed in a collection of the teachings given her, entitled *Reflections from an Angel's Eye*. Here is the vision of Soul and its incarnations as revealed by Francie's Parent-Guide:

Somewhere in space I stood suspended, and though the teachings was given in two minutes of our time, it seemed to me approximately fifteen to twenty minutes in total.

The picture that was given with the teaching was a living model. There was a "knowing" of that which they were showing. I was shown an area in the upper right-hand region of the picture and was told that it was the realm of the Hierarchy.

A golden cord extended from the realm; and I was told, and knew it to be, the umbilical cord that connects our Soul with that realm. At the end of the golden cord, there existed a large ball which I was told represented the Soul.

Extending from the Soul were many silver cords forming starlike rays which were umbilical cords that connected each life-form entered into with the Soul. At the end of every silver cord, approximately twelve shown, there existed smaller balls which I knew represented each lifetime on Earth.

Within each of these balls there formed an embryo which became a child and lived to an old age. While maturing, the life-form gathered knowledge, represented by lights around the form. Corresponding lights became incorporated as well, into the body known as the Soul, located in the hub of the model shown.

As the lights came to be within the Soul, the Soul expanded, and I "knew" its vibrations had increased from the knowledge gained by the life-forms. This continued with each form until all motion ceased. I was then told, by thought-form, that all souls would vibrate until they became a part of the Hierarchy once again. The Judgment that is to come will be of each lifetime lived. Some had raised their vibrations sufficiently and would be incorporated into the Soul and join it in its ascent to the Hierarchal domain, while others' lifetimes or areas shown became dark and ceased to continue to be alive or moving and never reached the Soul or the domain of the Hierarchy.

This, then, is the total teaching that accompanied the vision-teaching.

In the dimension now occupied by the Hierarchy, vibrations are of the highest frequency. At a period of time long since passed, all Souls began in this dimension, for it alone existed.

Possessing free will, many Souls lowered their vibrations. In so doing, they caused to exist another energy, a dimension of a lower frequency. They were thus divided from the Hierarchy, and the polarities of all things came to be.

All that exists is as a tapestry of varying colors or higher and lower frequencies. As a tapestry is of one thread throughout, so is life. Those Souls who lowered their vibrations are still joined to the Hierarchy by a golden thread, as an embryo is connected to its mother by an umbilical cord.

Unknown to the Souls, there existed a law of reality. This was that the lowering of a vibration is easier to accomplish than its raising. On Earth we, too, have become aware of this natural law. We realize it is far easier to fail than to excel, to expend effort to achieve a goal than to withdraw and accomplish nothing. An enlightening pictorial illustration of that law was given us when it was described that the path downward is wide and easy to tread, while the path up is narrow and more difficult.

Desiring only to return to the realm of the Hierarchy, the fallen Souls devised a plan. Sending forth an energy from their being, into a human life-form, in the realm of matter, they experienced life with its many events and gained wisdom. Since wisdom, or knowledge, is of a high vibrational frequency, being second only to love, they could thereby raise their vibrations. One day they would reach the level of the vibrations that exist in the Hierarchal realm and would return.

It is as it was: the Soul foresees all that might be gained in a particular life and sends forth a part of its energy into the embryonic life-form existing. It will then begin experiencing life, gathering the wisdom and love necessary to raise its vibrations.

Each life that our Soul chooses to enter is but a facet or personality of the Soul itself. That which the life-form encounters in the living out of its existence is "Soul-Chosen." When there is no longer any gaining to be had by the Soul, it withdraws its energy from the being or living facet of itself, thus removing its protective barrier. Upon the leaving of the Soul's energy, an inner part of our being begins vibrating at a higher frequency, while our physical bodies oscillate at a much lower rate than before. This threefold process is known as death.

In the beginning of human life, as we know it, there was created a male and female without knowledge or a future of any kind. In another domain there existed the Souls who had descended and were apart from the Hierarchal domain of other more highly vibrating Souls. Those descended, lower vibrating Souls realized that if they gave the male and female knowledge, they would cause the humans to raise their vibrations and, with knowledge, the humans would procreate their own kind, wherein the Souls could enter each life-form, experience life, and gain wisdom, thus increasing their vibrations. This was that which was told us in *Genesis* when the male and female ate of the tree of knowledge and "knew."

It was also written that the fallen souls interfered with that which was. However, it has rarely been realized that if they had not, we would not exist. Our Soul is one of the fallen Souls or descended Souls, which, through us, will one day return to the Hierarchy.

This, then, is the symbiotic relationship that exists between man and his Soul; the Soul needs us as much as we need it. We, too, as mere facets of our Soul, can become knowledgeable and be made more aware, thus increasing our vibrations so that we, too, may join our Soul in its ascent to the Hierarchal domain of higher vibrations.

Prophets, teachers, and inspired religious leaders have tried many times to enlighten mankind with this knowledge. Love and awareness raises our vibrations so that we might join our Soul and survive the death of matter.

All Souls will return to the Hierarchal domain. The judgment that is spoken of will be of the living facets or life-forms occupied by the Soul. It is we who will be judged.

Not all life-forms will become incorporated into the Soul and join it in its ascent. Some life-forms remained darkened and ceased to function or live, while others became bright with light. Those joined the brightened body of the Soul and all enlightened beings ascended to the Hierarchal realm.

I cannot say further of what might be the future of those beings who did not show forth light, for of them they spoke no further. I can only hope and pray they will not suffer, but that a plan might once again come into being that will raise their awareness so they, too, might join the Hierarchy.

As I came to know Francie better, I became increasingly pleased to find her down-to-earth, without being earthy. After all, one would not really like to discover that his "angel" had totally embraced the vibration of the material plane.

Refreshingly, I found her to be intensely mystical, without being muddled in mind; spiritual, without being tediously sanctimonious; highly moral, without being heavily judgmental of others; and serious in nature, without being devoid of a sense of humor.

I also found her to be a very practical person. Although I came to observe an incredible variety of paranormal phenomena occurring around her, Francie always tested and weighed each happening with the objective scrutiny of the scientist that she would have liked to have become.

"You remember what it was like in the fifties, Brad," she once complained. "I got A's in my science subjects, but my teacher advised me that, as a woman, my place was in the kitchen and to forget about college science courses."

I especially admired the manner in which Francie ceaselessly evaluates the teachings which are revealed to her. She scrupulously refuses to adapt the lessons to fit anyone's biases or confessional creeds. Nor does she at all desire to attempt analyses or interpretations of the teachings which might in any way inflate herself.

"I will only share the teachings as my Guardian Angel and my Parent-Guide have given them to me," she repeatedly emphasizes. "I will not add to them for purposes of my own ego—or anyone else's!"

In many ways I found Francie to be a sometimes perplexing study in contrasts.

She is an attractive blonde guru who seems immediately to inspire "followers" who insist that they cannot do without her almost continual guidance, but she demands that her students and clients become independent of her and that they learn to rely upon their own inner strengths.

She is a devoted mother, filled with old-fashioned love for her children, but she has reared them according to the dictates of her teachings and has made them understand that she is only their "Earth Mother," temporarily entrusted with their welfare and growth.

She is an exciting speaker and teacher, who must be entreated to abandon her reclusive, almost secretive, life-style for an occasional seminar or lecture-workshop.

There is no question that I was impressed with Francie—so much so that I married her.

Today, Francie is the principal channel for our Starbirth Foundation (7500 East Butherus Drive, Scottsdale, AZ 85260). She believes that what she is relaying is but an extension of the teachings from other worlds/dimensions which mankind has been receiving since ancient times.

"These teachings have always been designed to aid mankind in his quest for more fruitful, meaningful, peaceful lives," Francie commented. "It is obvious that the beings from this cosmic, celestial Hierarchy have long ago assumed a parental attitude toward humanity and that they have long employed a system of education in dealing with us.

"These teachings are universal in nature," she went on, "and I have received instructions on the ways in which mankind may make contact with the Hierarchy so that each individual may accomplish his or her own guidance and channel his own teachings.

"All have within them the ability to contact and to reach the Hierarchy. We must always remember that the Temple of God lies within each one of us."

CHAPTER EIGHT:
PAST LIVES THROUGH ALTERED STATES OF CONSCIOUSNESS

For the past five years, a slender, attractive blonde named Susan Harris has been researching reincarnation through past-life regressions which she accomplished by the use of certain suggestive techniques. Together with her tall, broad-shouldered husband Jay, Susan edits *The Psychic Gazette* (P.O. Box 2145, Scottsdale, AZ 85252) and is a coordinator of the Advanced Psychical Research Association. They are a friendly, pleasant couple, eager to share information and observations on the entire psychic scene.

When I asked Susan to share some of her most interesting research cases with us, she readily agreed, adding: "I feel that the altered states of consciousness reached through certain techniques which I have developed offer an extremely fertile ground for investigation of reincarnation. Most of my really interesting cases occur in private counseling sessions, but I have also had a number of exciting cases develop during my public demonstrations."

Susan began her sharing of past-life regressions with an account of a subject who happened to have been chosen from about 120 men and women who had gathered for one of her public demonstrations of altered states of consciousness. The most outstanding point of this case, according to Susan, was the fact that the subject's sense of life-flow continuity seemed totally out of order and kept everyone wondering until the end of the demonstration just what would come of the puzzling disorder. I'll permit Susan to continue her account in her own words:

After I had released the man to a creative level of visualization, the subject, whom I'll call Ray, described his skeletal body. In my technique, I instruct the subject to view his feet first. We all know what our feet look like; and it doesn't take such imagination on the part of the subject to begin the visualization, then move up his physical body to describe the clothing and gain an idea of the period of time, his or her sex, and so forth. Most subjects follow this suggestion easily, but in Ray's case I could not in any way anticipate what he was doing.

Telepathically, I could see that he was indeed looking at an entire skeleton in an open grave. I suggested possibly he was an archeologist digging up bones, but Ray continued on and described a claylike texture that was being molded and shaped into a head and a face. (No! He was not a sculptor.)

The next thing Ray described was himself, kneeling on the floor of a cage. He was inside looking through the bars at people looking in at him. In the corner was a gorilla, lazily tossing a feeding dish and watching Ray out of the corner of his eye. It seemed as though it might be Ray's job to clean its cage.

There is opportunity for humor in these demonstrations, and someone from the audience mentioned something about, "Now we know who cleaned the bottom of Noah's Ark!"

It seemed as though Ray was never going to come out of that cage! When he did, he was busily strapping on funny red clothlike shoes that had turned-up toes with bells on them. They were small enough to fit a child's foot. When I asked what he was doing, Ray described the shoes in a tone that sharply suggested that I should know what he was doing since he goes bouncing off like a court jester all the time!

At this point I honestly thought I had chosen a real nut from an audience of 120 people. One could see this strange, little, dwarflike man, bouncing down a cobblestone street in a setting of approximately seventeenth-century Europe, with an entire parade behind him.

Then the pieces finally began to fit together in this bizarre scene. The circus had come to town! The townspeople had lined both sides of the narrow street watching the performers in their colorful costumes march by, as the horse-drawn animal wagons brought up the rear.

The confusion was that Ray had viewed the entire incarnation in reverse, seemingly from the deterioration of the body, molding it back to the physical life, and finally to the bottom of the gorilla cage. Apparently the gorilla had been in a nasty mood that particular day and had taken it out on his keeper and killed him. The point is that no matter what I suggested he might be, Ray persisted in seeing what actually took place in his memory, and he was not in the least detracted by my suggestions.

One of the most beneficial uses of this technique, in my opinion, is that the individual has an opportunity to view himself/herself objectively and subjectively. It is much safer to view another person "saying the wrong things" or being clumsy and uncoordinated, especially if there are repercussions brought forth in this incarnation from another lifetime.

The law of cosmic requital for one's good and bad deeds is known as Karma. One is believed to take breath, die, and be reborn again and again until his slate is clean of any debt and the soul reaches a balance. The following case study is what I categorize as "classical" in my research.

This client came to his decision to have a past-life regression after having checked out all medical reasons for his particular handicap. He had a limitation in the use of his right arm. Occasionally, the arm would not function properly, and it would just go limp.

He claimed that he could not be hypnotized, and when the session began, I partially understood why. The gentleman's concentration was, at best, a span of thirty seconds. His mind would zip around like a butterfly, never quite landing anywhere.

This fellow was not only skeptical about the regression, but he also insulted the level of sensitivity, calling it a "con." Obviously, it was difficult for him to relax and let go of his reasoning.

His comments continued with, "I'm a writer myself. I can sit here all day and make up stories for you!"

I instructed him to do so. He gave a few, glib short stories, one having to do with a Confederate soldier, another with a detective. I don't mind admitting that after a few of these fantasies, my patience was about to go out the window.

Finally he began to show some emotion about a particular scene, which he started describing. This small-framed man of seemingly mild mannerisms began visualizing a huge, muscular Roman soldier of questionable character with an ear-to-ear grin that would make anyone wonder about his motives. He was wearing a tunic with leather straps that protected the body. In his left hand he held a shield, and with his right hand, he was flailing a large silver sword that caught the sunlight as he swung it in front of him. He was ruthless, and he snarled at defenseless people to "move on!"

The entire scene was one of a Roman arena. Dust was flying as people fell over each other, pushing their way past this soldier with the sword. People began screaming and crying out as several lions ran excitedly into the arena from openings in the walls.

There was a sense of power and pride in the voice that was relating this scene. He even boastfully numbered the thousands of people he had forced to their death. He saw his life pass before him with a clear recollection of his name as the head of a legion of trained men.

Since he still had no sense of remorse, I instructed him to view his death in that incarnation. He described his reactions as the breath of life left him and his body became limp and still. His sensations were as though something filmlike had lifted from the body, and he described a pulling sensation at the chest.

For what seemed like a full two minutes he was silent, and there was no communication. Suddenly, he reacted with a deep sigh, releasing emotions that seemed to come from the very depths of his being. As he wept openly, his words were, "I made an agreement, a promise in spirit, to use my right arm only after weighing the outcome of my actions in that lifetime."

Today, this man has little difficulty with his right arm. The understanding of the agreement did not necessarily cure him. It gave him reasons for the limitation. As long as he upholds his end of the bargain, he is free of this limitation.

The next case study is classfiied as more of a psychological carry-over, rather than a physical Karma.

Through a conscious effort to release himself of felinophobia, his fear of cats, my client had previously undergone extensive psychiatric treatment. There had to be a distinct origin for his abnormal behavior. There had to be reasons why a man of six feet, three inches, weighing 200 pounds, felt panic and froze at the sight of a cat.

It was found that his mother had kept several cats in the house. When he was eighteen months old, one of the cats found its way into the child's nursery and crept into his crib.

The child was terrified as this little animal moved from his feet to his chest and stared into his very own eyes.

He screamed, thrashing wildly at the animal to get it away from him.

It must have been hours before the boy responded to his own mother. When they found the baby, after hearing his screams, he was stiff and rigid and his eyes were staring without seeing anything in front of him.

His dreams from that time on were nightmares of cats with flaring nostrils, coming right up close to his own face to take his breath away.

Having triggered this memory through hypnosis, his previous doctors had been satisfied that this incident had been the reason for the man's fear and that the dreams would subside. But the next time my client had come across a cat in the same room with him, he had reacted even more violently than before.

He seemed to sense their presence by some uncanny power of the mind. He could not only hear them, but he could also "feel" the throaty purr of a cat when others in the same room were not even aware of a cat's presence. The only explanation his therapists could give him was that "out of habit, he had become obsessed with the 'idea' of cats coming to harm him."

During the regression, I had guided him to sense only the presence of animals, viewing them objectively so as not to shock or to overstimulate the emotions to a waking state of consciousness before any understanding was achieved.

I had suggested a point in time that would directly relate to the problem at hand. As he drifted deeper . . . and deeper . . . asleep . . . he began to visualise stone temples, huge pyramids, a vast, dry desert and, finally, there was a path that led to his dwelling. The description of the courtyard was vivid, and the interior was detailed right to the tapestry on the wall.

He was of a high Egyptian family, not of the Pharaohs, but one of stature all the same. His father had a position in which he judged cases of a lower than diplomatic status, but which were important to the merchant and businessman of that time.

The sixteen-year-old boy had already been trained in many diplomatic matters. He stated that all boys of his class were schooled in this manner to prepare them for positions they would be expected to handle as adults. This day in particular was one of celebration, as the class had graduated to another school of even more intense training.

Everyone was there. He could see some of the people who are in his life today, and many who seemed familiar.

As the people became noisy and the music was drowned out by their laughter, the boy moved out into the courtyard. This was one of his favorite places. It was quiet; the plants and flowers of the garden offered a coolness and fragrance no other place could. From the terrace, only a few steps out of the garden, he could view the entire city, just a little below the house.

To his right he watched the sky and water meet in brilliant colors of the sunset. It was silent but for the distant music from the party.

His eyes followed the path just below the terrace to the small temple which stored the family treasures. A high fence surrounded this sacred temple, and its gate was ajar. He thought of the cat that guarded it from intruders! Suddenly, he felt a crawly, electrified feeling go through his body, from his heels to the top of his head.

A low, purring sound seemed to echo off the walls of his skull. From the bushes behind him, two eyes shown, piercing like two lights glimmering in a black velvet head. Without a sound, without any warning, the cat leaped as though defying all laws of gravity, instantly killing its prey.

A peaceful warmth came over the boy's entire body. As his spirit lifted up and away from this scene, he watched the cat gracefully move away, back to the temple.

Some people would say that this is a horrifying experience to relive; but to my client, it was a relief, an explanation which gave an understanding to his reactive behavior.

This experience did not cure him! He still doesn't like cats, but he no longer fears them. In this past experience there was justification for the fears which had stayed with him. The sounds and emotions became warnings to him and carried over into this incarnation.

It is my personal belief that when an individual reaches altered states of consciousness, he is experiencing a "no time" reality. This is why it is termed "altered"; it is out of the general concepts of time. One can view situations and circumstances which have already occurred, touching into memory, as well as things of the future. I believe that this is the space a psychic or clairvoyant attempts to reach, and many times is successful when "reading" an individual.

More and more people are reaching into this space of awareness, and finding an ability in their natural sensitivity to display clairvoyance, telepathy, precognition, etc. This is something they may have been doing all of their lives. The difference now is the awareness of what they are doing and their learning how to repeat it. Generally, one could say, man is becoming multidimensional in his being. He is able to look backward, forward, and in the process become totally aware of the "now" within himself. This does not imply that the multi-aware person cannot function within the everyday three-dimensional level of consciousness. On the contrary, this individual not only functions more creatively than ever before, but also finds that he is not limited by the concepts of three-dimensional "time."

Many of the people who are viewing things of the future through progression are finding that this technique allows them to be more objective and to see all of the choices to any given situation. Some of the events viewed seem far into the future.

The following case study is a good example of "altered time" in a progression. In this research study, the progression was documented and found to be evidential and precise to the smallest detail.

Diane is a counselor for a large firm. She is twenty-seven years of age, married, and has one child. Having effectively suggested and relaxed Diane to the state of visualization, the scene was clearly recorded as she entered her home. This had to be a new home, one in the future, as it was unfamiliar to her.

The living room was spacious, approximately 15 x

20. The windows allowed a lot of light into the room. The carpet was a pale yellow color, short shag texture. Diane's attitude was one resembling a shopper looking at a model home, and it was fun to go through a house with no one else there! The bedrooms were also an even color, but there were strong earth tones of orange and brown in decorative bedspreads and curtains. Both baths in the house were large with double sinks, and the master bath had a sunken tub with a glass exposure where plants received sunlight through a window in the ceiling. She moved down the hall and into the family room, three steps down, and viewed a beautiful fireplace that extended the entire wall with a light colored stone.

As Diane turned, she started getting what I call a "double exposure." She saw a Grecian archway, columns, and a scene of a garden. Occasionally, a subject will trigger memory by another memory and parallel one scene with another that doesn't seem to fit in that incarnation.

Looking through the arcadia doors and into the backyard, Diane described three dog runs and fences that breeders use to exercise their animals across the entire yard. At the other end of the yard were six doghouses.

Diane explained to me later that she and her husband Jim raise show dogs for competition, and it is her desire to someday build dog runs. Diane felt that this house would be just perfect for them, but she also knew that this was at least ten years away. This appeared far more expensive than they could afford in the near future.

Exactly three days after the progression, Diane contacted me about a house she was going to see. A real estate friend of theirs had, on occasion, tried to get them to view different houses, even though they were not looking for a new home. Because of the progression, Diane felt compelled to follow up on this offer.

Upon entering the house, Diane described that eerie feeling of having been there before. The house was precisely the same one she had previewed. The only discrepancy was that there was a design in the carpeting of the family room.

As she was looking at the fireplace and turned to her left, she saw what had given her the double exposure in the altered state of consciousness. There on the entire wall was a mural of a Grecian garden, complete with archways and columns. The backyard was as she had seen it, with the doghouses and the three dog runs.

Six weeks later to the day, Diane and her family moved into the very house she had previewed less than two months before. As it turned out the price was right, the owners were also real estate people and listed Diane's home for them, and it was not as far out of reach financially as she had anticipated.

The progression itself was a very timely occurrence in bringing about some of Diane's dreams. It did not make it happen; it simply helped Diane to be alert to things that were about to happen to her. One thing for certain: the progression made believers out of Diane and her family.

This is not an uncommon instance. Many people view their next job, possibly a future home, and often new people coming into their lives through this technique. I have had many people ask, "How can we view something that hasn't happened yet?"

The best answer I can give is: "Is this really much different from viewing something in memory out of the past?"

For the multidimensional person—the flexible individual who is subject to, but not limited by, this concept of time between sunrise and sunset—there is a space I call "no time." Some of the technical information being researched and collected today is fascinating, and there may be truth to the concepts of the "Atlantean crystals" and some of their functions. Some subjects are tuning in to principles having to do with space travel, which may have a very strong influence on future travel.

We are finding practical uses in our three-dimensional world for techniques which were once thought of as being merely parlor games and entertainment. We are finding information having to do with the origin of man on this planet, as well as discovering physical artifacts and evidence to prove the accuracy of our information.

Is there anything to the expression, "The Aquarian Age is the Age of Awareness"? As man uses his sensitivities, his spiritual creative energy, is he just now becoming a multidimensional being in a three-dimensional world? Or is he moving on to a fourth, or higher, dimension?

I believe this to be the case. As I continue my research, I hope one day to be able to prove that we are naturally raising our vibrations to a higher frequency. This could mean that we are preparing a new world here on Earth, a new vibration—or we are preparing to move to another world with another vibration.

CHAPTER NINE:
TWO METAPHYSICIANS DISCUSS REINCARNATION

Some metaphysicians believe that there exists what are called the Akashic Records, eternal accountings of individual life patterns which have been somehow impressed on etheral mechanisms. These records detail each lifetime and are perpetuated like vast computer-like memory banks in the collective unconscious. Certain gifted individuals may, in altered states of consciousness, rise above the normal limitations of Time and Space and "read" these past lives. When they return to the mundane world, they may recount these memories in such a way as to aid men and women who seek their counsel to avoid certain errors which were committed in earlier lifetimes.

Kingdon L. Brown, a nationally recognized psychic, author of *The Power of Psychic Awareness* and *Cosmosis,* is said to have the ability to "tune in" on the Akashic Records. In July 1977, I had the opportunity to renew an old friendship with Kingdon at his Desert Shadows Church of Essential Science in Scottsdale, Arizona.

I began our conversation by teasing Kingdon a bit about the description of him in Alan Weisman's *We, Immortals:* "Almost portly, bespectacled, looking about forty or so, his shirt cuffs a little too short, Kingdon Brown's aura . . . was more that of someone's pleasant, candy-giving uncle than that of a spiritual medium."

Then, moving from the jocular to the complimentary, Weisman writes: "I decided that if Kingdon Brown were as gifted a psychic as he is a public speaker, it would probably be worth the money to have one's fortune read by him. His tone is even-keeled, and intentionally undramatic. . . . Unlike most others I've seen on the cosmic lecture circuit, Kingdon Brown eschews historians in favor of simplicity, flowing smoothly and lucidly from topic to topic. . . ."

Eventually our dialogue got around to survival of the spirit in general and reincarnation in particular. Here, edited for publication, are a number of the topics which we discussed that day:

Brad Steiger: How did you begin to realize that you were attuning to the Akashic Records while doing psychic counseling?

Kingdon Brown: Much of what I would "see" seemed to be symbolic, a different time and place, perhaps, as if I had attuned to a dream. Several clients suggested that this material might be of former lifetimes and relationships. Slowly I began to accept this explanation and tried to gain greater detail with this type of visual feeling. Later, in many cases, my psychic impression was verified by a hypnotic regression. In other cases a new love-person came into the life of my client, who had also a vague recollection of having been in a previous lifetime with that individual. Often these relationships blossomed to the point of forming a new marriage, a new permanence.

Do you have a general theory about how reincarnation seems to work?

I can only recite some of the usual theories and add a few observations of my own. I am continuing to discover possibilities, new mechanical ways the soul seems to progress from its point of creation. I think we do exist in a cosmic scheme that is orderly, logical, and predictable. But the paranormal experience suggests to me that we do not know all there is to know about just how our universe is organized or why we are here to understand people whom we seem to attract to ourselves. In retrospect it appears that all experiences seem to be programmed, seem to fit into an overall scheme of which we are only partially aware.

I have often wondered if we do not all undergo similar experiences in one lifetime or another under the guise of new times and places. It seems that there may be a universal pathway that we follow. Maybe our experiences, reactions, and relationships are interchangeable, actually symbolic themselves, even though they seem to be firmly rooted in physical reality.

To say that all of this is designed to allow us to grow into our full potential, our divine-human combination, is not explanation enough. The process of the soul's growth and self-awareness of its presence and growth, of its influence over our present experience pattern, is complex indeed.

But, there are some strange repeating situations.

One conclusion that I would reach is that most evolving souls, those who are coming to an idea of self that is universal and not personal, rarely continue one basic marriage throughout a lifetime. Most often they seem to create new intimate relationships as they reach new stages of growth and greater levels of complex awareness.

The most common pattern here is a fundamental marriage, usually in the early twenties, that appears to have as its purpose the creation of new biological entities—children. Then, there is a time when these children approach early maturity, their own early-twenties time, that a "crisis" occurs in a marriage. Suddenly the duo finds that they are actually moving along separate pathways in life, have different needs, and may require new partners. There is the need, at this point, to share new breakthroughs in consciousness with another soul who may be searching for a higher, more universal, less egocentric meaning. The very inner stress of this type of turning point brings into play Karmic memories, haunting ideas of the ideal mate, of a better time and place, of something slightly out of kilter about present reality, of Earth as it now is.

And, sure enough, without a lot of prompting in most cases, as if by an unseen plan, the new mate comes into view.

Are you saying, then, that one of the central meanings of reincarnation is for various souls to interact and exchange energies somehow?

If humankind is going to advance to the place where we can live on this planet in peace and harmony, with a sense of balance and inner poise, we must share our insights and feelings in most intimate circumstances. Otherwise we can look forward to a future, like the past, that is warlike, greedy, destructive.

Are people sometimes surprised by what may be revealed?

For some the idea that they have had past lifetimes as women and as men is shattering. Evidently for these people their identity is firmly fixed in what they see as male or female roles, as mother or father. Thus, when they come upon the concept that they have played many roles, it stops them cold. Then, upon reflection they find that, even now, they have both masculine and feminine characteristics. I personally think that this androgynous nature of ourselves makes it easier for men and women to relate successfully. They see something familiar, yet different, in each other. If our purpose were simply to create new biological persons, we would probably get together just to mate and then depart until "next year's" mating season, as other life-forms do.

As it is, there is an intrinsic purpose, an overwhelming quality to more meaningful relationships that takes the simple biological union, sex, into a transcendental experience, a feeling of totality, or union with the divine. In these rare instances, the male and female energies of each party are co-joined and euphoria results.

As we come into the Aquarian Age, of course, this means we have many types of intimate relationships available, many different life-styles, more room for difference and diversity. That automatically breeds a tolerance for the other fellow, for his needs, at his particular stage of growth.

Are these stages of personal growth and evolution as pre-programmed as you claim? Or are there alternative explanations?

I don't think they come in one, two, three order. We seem to move three steps forward and two back. The blending is beautifully random and not as controlled as one might think at first glance.

I also have a feeling for "soul groups." That is, there seems to be people who have a marvelous affinity for each other because their background of experiences seems to be similar, seems to have brought them to similar points of conclusion.

It is amazing to me that so *many people* who feel that reincarnation is a good explanation for our cause-and-effect experience creations have lived in ancient times. *Very few* to whom reincarnation is valid were around on this planet during the time between about 700 A.D.-1500 A.D.

Maybe the idea of reincarnation is only acceptable to those who intuitively feel that they have lived before. To others the NOW is the principal reality.

I'd sum up Karma as: "What we need is what we get!"

What about the idea that we live in an Eternal Now, and that we simply tend to view it as happening in a literal time-space way when it is really a gigantic three-dimensional chessboard, filled with parallel selves, multiple selves, and so on.

The concept of the Akashic Records is that they are available now, that everything that has happened, maybe everything that is going to happen, does exist in another reality, in a different dimension of reality.

But I personally find the idea of multiple selves coming in all over the place as a little confusing. I don't see the practicality of this concept for me. But, of course, it might be very helpful to others.

My world, however, is peopled with spiritual entities, souls, who, I think, are available for the spirit side of life. I have investigated the whole question of life after death, and I do not have any problem communicating with souls that are in the afterlife. Perhaps for some people the idea of multiple selves serves the same purpose as Guides and Teachers for the spiritualist. If an idea works for you, use it. If it doesn't, forget it for now.

Frankly, it is a little frightening to me to think that I've got some multiple parts of me still hanging around. I've got enough to do just figuring me out as I seem right this minute. To each his own.

Why, do you suppose, people come to you to check into their past lifetimes?

The overwhelming question is what is my purpose in the present lifetime and am I fulfilling it?

People are interested in reincarnation to gain some glimpse of their sense of unease, of causes to a lack of fulfillment and harmony. Also, many people that I meet feel that there is a mission to which they should respond. They are literally overcoming more rigid views of the selfhood; they want to dedicate themselves to something meaningful, purposeful, and transcendent. This is not confined to any one age group, or any single social category. It is a common thread throughout America.

Second to personal relationship questions is this curiosity about life purpose, mission, and direction.

Can you reach any conclusions about life directions? Is there something that many people see in common as their purpose?

The most striking common characteristic is the surprise that many people evidence as they approach a major turning point in life. A death of a loved one, a divorce, or change of occupation are obvious ones. But evidently there are other, more subtle, inner changes of values, priorities, life-styles, and psychological needs that prompt an investigation of past-life influences.

In other words, many people reach a point in their self-awareness when they ask, "Is this all there is?"

Or, to put it another way, many have set their lives into molds, assuming that they have everything "figured out," only to find that their assumptions are outmoded, that they are in a different state of self-sensitivity; the personal world has changed and they must adapt. As they adjust to new circumstances, new levels of awareness, there are discoveries of one's inner world.

I think what we are seeing is a discovery of a higher selfhood, a more universal, less restricted, personal identity. This causes uncertainty and doubt at first, of course. But, a tolerance for ambiguity is evidently one of the signs of personal growth and evidence that a more fulfilling life is coming into being.

This stage requires an inquiring mind, a nonjudgmental, open attitude and faith that there is something to be gained, a new potential to be realized, lived, enjoyed.

Reincarnation answers the quandry for many people; it erases the unease, the lack of purpose. It replaces these feelings with new adventure, hope, and, above all, places the individual in touch with aspects of his own personality and being that may have been hidden.

There is the understanding, too, that all humankind is alike in many ways; we all sense the same joys, fears, hopes, and aspirations through many lifetimes.

Since reincarnation deals with the history of the soul, what do you find in the attitude of traditional religions on this subject?

Strangely enough, most people do not see an investigation of reincarnation as having anything to do with their traditional religious affiliation. This might surprise most clergymen. I think this is because once a person has grown into a feeling of universal truth, he or she may view traditional church concepts as nearly useless, simply a form of truth, a window on some aspects of life, and not rigid, dogmatic, or doctrine-clad.

A seeker after truth will simply ignore those theological constructs that are not relevant to his discovery. A student of reincarnation may not be anti-religious, but he is probably willing to overlook the incongruities of organized religion in favor of an ever-changing spirituality.

Some are able to maintain an active religious affiliation that they see in a more symbolic light. Religion may be more like an art form than like a specific science.

Students of reincarnation are open to new ideas, are willing to sacrifice self-concepts for a higher, more satisfying diversity of experience. While a crisis may have prompted the original inquiry into the subject, a steady balance soon emerges and often new paranormal insights dawn.

We are still faced with how previous life influences draw individuals, particularly those in love relationships, together. Many feel there are times of release when previous soul ties are fulfilled and new freedom of relationship choice comes forward.

We find that marriage partners, for instance, often find themselves moving in different directions. A new relationship with another partner presents itself as a strong possibility. The new partner may have a "feel" for the *subject* of previous lifetimes, may "sense" an inward draw to the soul to be released from a marriage. Hence, a new bond is born out of the distant past and is less explained by traditional psychology, or present life facts. Two people are magnetized to one another for reasons which are not easily articulated out of the present, but which have their origins in a past association, sometimes dimly recollected.

Many people whom I have counseled about their own past lives have felt that the Earth plane is not where reality is. They have felt uncomfortable with the entire game of Earth life. And they talk about another plane in the universe that seems more like home. We may not be outcasts sent to Earth. We may be "missionaries" placed here to seed a new consciousness for mankind.

Many people sense lives, then, on other planets, at

other places in the universe. They have no difficulty feeling an extra-dimensional life, of communicating with "unseen" forces and entities.

One of the most respected metaphysicians in the Chicago area is Deon Frey Scudamore, a gifted interpreter of the Tarot and an advanced practitioner of True Magick by way of the ancient Mystery Schools. I have know Deon for more than a decade, and I have been priviledged to share her wisdom and knowledge in a number of my previous works. It seemed only fitting that I should ask her to contribute thoughts on reincarnation for this present volume. Herewith is Deon's teaching:

I dedicate this work to the Soul of the universal world. The workings of the universe are ofttimes beyond our comprehension; yet we know within our minds that we are led on the path up the Tree of Life toward a universal truth—that the Soul grows throughout eternity . . . no beginning, no end. So the age-old question—do we live on?—has little meaning to our inner selves.

Some demand a proof of reincarnation. They want to see it broken down into a formula, just as we can add two plus two to equal four. Whenever I think of the multiplication tables, I always ponder why they cease with 12 x 12 equals 144. Is there a deeper significance to this final multiplication?

The Earth planet is not my home. I only stopped by here a while in Time in order to counteract some ideas that I must have once needed to believe and in order to meet and somehow to touch the lives of those who are important to my auric circle of being.

We each have an auric circle—or egg-shaped light

fixation—that we carry with us into each incarnation. I believe that in each incarnation we have a similar body, perhaps made of different atoms of light. We, ourselves, are atoms which were exploded into being from the beginning of Time.

Perhaps many of the so-called "stars" that blink down on you at night are contributing parts of the great light carried by each Soul from the beginning of Time. We will all go one day to make up the great Central Sun. Each Soul-star could be projecting a light back to Earth for another Soul to follow its course through the Heavens. Many of the objects called UFOs might be clusters of atoms manifesting together to travel to other planets and places in the universe.

Will I, Deon, incarnate again? No, not here on Earth. But, yes, I will incarnate anew in some other solar system in order to fulfill my mission, which is eternal. My ego shall have slipped away, and I will become all love and understanding so that I may become anew in a spiritual body in union with self.

As I look into the mirror of life, I see a great era of understanding in each bubble in the ocean of existence. I will become the two plus two here, or I will square the circle and become one with the four plus three and go to the apex of the triangle to learn the secrets and the wisdom of the ages.

One of the greatest secrets is to keep traveling on and to learn from everyone we touch. We pick up a portion of each vibration or atom we touch. Sometimes we darken our light by accepting wrong ideas or thoughts. Let us take each thought and divide it, separate it, and then multiply it as it seems to fit our lives.

I choose to believe in a rebirth of the Soul's growth in a new body of life wherever it might be. Perhaps as we bring together the different atoms, we mold our Star Body. In the 12 x 12 around the Zodiac of life, we grow in the circle of perfection by becoming a part of each zodiacal sign in the 144,000 times we return or are reborn in a different position of Time.

As we come to feel with our inner selves, we experience the entirety of life's growth. Our Soul comes to realize itself, and we give in return to it. Glow without as you glow within, and forever move as your atom shines somewhere.

As I prepared to enter planet Earth, I gathered my flow of light stars together in order to enter the "S" shape of force that flows together to force the atoms into life's expression. As the ball of light bounces forth, it enters into the expression of life through the love of attraction and two forces, negative and positive, man and woman. We are able to heal through the negative force by bringing it back into the positive force so we must use the inner flow of the forces.

My mission here on Earth is to brighten the light of my Star. I have the capacity to alter the light of the Star parallel to mine and so do you! When I sense that something is wrong with another, I want to know why. I use my Star body to become aware of the problem and to learn what I can do to help. Once I have this awareness, I will know how another feels, and I will hope to alter his or her problem in some way. If he has a headache, I will feel it until I remove myself—and, hopefully, the pain—from his flow of light.

We all possess Star bodies. If you misuse your Star body of your light flow, you become a dark star with little or no light shining forth.

Your Star body contacts the magnetic field of each other Star body, as magnets attract or reject the different polarities. The key is to fill your magnetic self with positive action and send it into a negative Star body so that the light will be renewed.

Star bodies undulate, spin, and attract. This is the reason we have out-of-body experiences. We go into an internal spin so that we can reach back into space. Our mental Star body challenges everything we experience in order to set us spinning.

We use each other in our pattern of life in order to reinforce our magnetic fields. The essence of the Star body is body-mind-spirit. Our memory is retained in our Star body, but sometimes we almost shatter it with our thoughts and our actions. As a result of our reason, we often try to test our thoughts, not realizing that all thought-forms become reality as we project them into space.

We become the living records of our own life, and we play the "music" over and over, trying to hear the blessed "Music of the Spheres," which is the harmony of life's spinning action and the rubbing together of each Star body.

The Space Brothers call me "Donna." The Universal Magi Temple calls me High Priestess Judith. The 109-year-old Hopi Chief Dan Katchongwa called me Sienma, "Little Pumpkin." A true friend I chanced to meet on this Earth plane hailed me as "Donna Rae." (We must have met before. Our recognition was instant!) My father named me Deon, for the God of light.

Life is a mystery that is open to us only if we use our Star bodies to project to other worlds to find out the answers for ourselves. We are chained to life by the links of our Star bodies to each other. There is a universal pulse beat, just as we have ours.

I am a mystic, traveling through space on the road

to perfection so that I may be taught by the Masters of Life, those who have attained the perfection which we all seek.

You, Brad Steiger, are my Space Brother. We have been together in many incarnations. Francie I have also known many times. Our Star bodies have touched, and we have worked together. My love reaches out to you and yours and the work to be accomplished by your Starbirth Foundation. I shall not long be with you here, but our Star bodies will always touch and we will work together elsewhere. So must it be as we travel onward and upward to distant stars, stars of blazing light.

CHAPTER TEN:
BRIDEY MURPHY REVISITED

To a great number of Americans, "Bridey Murphy" has become synonymous with reincarnation. This story of the Pueblo, Colorado, housewife who remembered a past life while under hypnosis made a dramatic impact upon the public imagination. Newspapers, magazines, and scholarly journals debated the validity of the "memory," and controversy surrounding this alleged case of reincarnation has not resolved itself to this day.

William J. Barker of the *Denver Post* published the first account of this now-famous case in that newspaper's *Empire* magazine. Barker told how Morey Bernstein, a young Pueblo business executive, first noticed what an excellent subject "Mrs. S." was for deep trance when he was asked to demonstrate hypnosis at a party in October of 1952.

It was some weeks later, on the evening of November 29, that Bernstein gained the woman's consent to participate in an experiment of age-regression.

The amateur hypnotist had heard stories of men who had led their subjects back into past lives, but he had always scoffed at such tales. He had been particularly skeptical about the testimony of the British psychiatrist Sir Alexander Cannon, who reported that he had investigated over a thousand cases wherein entranced individuals had recalled past incarnations.

Mrs. S., who later became identified as Ruth Simmons, was not particularly interested in hypnotism nor in becoming a guinea pig for Bernstein's attempt to test the thesis of Cannon and the others who had claimed investigation of former lives. She was, at that time, twenty-eight years old, an attractive young matron who enjoyed playing bridge and attending ball games with her husband. Mrs. S. was, to employ a Madison Avenue cliché, the typical American housewife.

With Mr. Simmons and Mrs. Bernstein as witnesses, the hypnotist began to lead Mrs. Simmons back through significant periods of her childhood. Finally, it was time for the big try.

Bernstein placed Mrs. Simmons in a trance, then told her that she was going back until she found herself in another time and another place. The hypnotist told his subject that she would be able to talk to him and tell him what she saw.

Bernstein paused for a glass of water, waited another minute or two before he spoke again to Mrs. Simmons.

When he asked her if she could view a scene from an earlier existence, the woman began to breathe heavily. Her first words from an alleged previous memory were more enigmatic than dramatic.

"I'm scratching the paint off my bed, because I'm mad. I had just got an awful spankin'!"

When Bernstein asked for the personality's name and was told "Bridey Murphy," the strange search for evidence of a former incarnation had begun.

At first, though, the hypnotist-businessman was unimpressed with his subject's apparent memory of a former existence in Ireland, because "strange responses often come from people under hypnosis."

Then Bridey—short for Bridget—began to use words and expressions that were completely out of character for Mrs. Simmons. And, as Mr. Simmons pointed out, more than simply being out of character, the use of certain terms required a knowledge which his "ordinary" wife did not, or could not, possess.

Bridey told of playing hide'n'seek with her brother Duncan, who had "reddish hair like mine" (Mrs. Simmons was a brunette).

She told of attending Mrs. Strayne's school in Cork where she spent her time "studying to be a lady."

With sensitivity she re-created her marriage to Brian MacCarthy, a young lawyer, who took her to live in Belfast in a cottage back of his grandmother's house, not far from St. Theresa's church.

In her melodic brogue, "Bridey Murphy" told of a life without children, a life laced with a small point of conflict because she was Protestant while Brian was Catholic; then, in a tired and querulous voice, she told them how she had fallen down a flight of stairs when she was sixty-six.

After her fall, Bridey had had to be carried about. The burden was lifted one Sunday when she died while Brian was at church. It upset him terribly, Bridey said. She recalled how she lingered beside her husband, trying to establish communication with him, trying to let him know that he should not grieve for her.

"People on earth won't listen," she complained.

Bridey told the astonished hypnotist and his witnesses that she had waited around Belfast until Father John, a priest friend of her husband's, had passed away. She wanted to point out to him that he was wrong about purgatory, she said, and added that he admitted it.

The spirit world, she said, was one in which you couldn't talk to anybody very long . . . they'd go away. One did not sleep, never ate, and never became tired. Bridey thought that she had lived in the spirit realm for about forty years before she was reborn as Mrs. Simmons.

At a second session, Bridey again stressed that the "afterlife" was painless, nothing to be afraid of. There was neither love nor hate, and relatives did not stay together in clannish groups.

Her father, she recalled, said he saw her mother, but she didn't.

The spirit world, then, was simply a place where the soul waited to pass on to "another form of existence."

Details of Bridey Murphy's physical life on earth began to amass on Morey Bernstein's tape recorders. Business associates who heard the tapes encouraged Bernstein to continue with his experiments but to let someone else, a disinterested third party, check Bridey's statements in old Irish records or wherever such evidence might be found.

Ruth Simmons was not eager to continue with the series of experiments, but the high regard which both she and her husband had for Morey Bernstein led her to consent to submit to additional sessions.

Bernstein told *Empire* magazine that he made careful notes in preparation for each session after the personality of Bridey Murphy had revealed itself.

The hypnotist stressed the importance of avoiding loaded questions in dealing with an entranced person. The subject becomes childlike in that he will be disposed to say what he thinks the hypnotist wants him to say.

During each session, additional "evidence" of her existence was given to the researchers by the charming Irishwoman.

She recalled how her mother had told her stories of the Irish Hercules, Cuchulain the warrior.

Utilizing the body of Mrs. Simmons, Bridey demonstrated a graceful and lively rendition of an Irish folk dance which she called "the Morning Jig." Her favorite songs were learned to be "Sean," "The Ministrel's March," and "The Londonderry Air." Mrs. Simmons had no interest in musical activities previously.

Barker asked Morey Bernstein if he felt the strange case of Bridey Murphy could be explained by memory which had been transferred through Mrs. Simmons' ancestors.

The young hypnotist-businessman conceded that the whole episode would make a better story if it could be proved that Bridey Murphy were one of Mrs. Simmons' forebears. The subject was one-third Irish, but the genetic memory hypothesis falls apart when it is remembered that Bridey had no children.

Other researchers who have regressed subjects back into previous life-memories have found that blood line and heredity have nothing to do with former incarnations. Many have spoken of the afterlife as a kind of "stockpile of souls." When a particular type of spirit is required to inhabit and animate a body that is about to be born, that certain spirit is selected and introduced into that body.

Bernstein observed frankly and humorously that a person who boasts of having noble French ancestry may have been an African slave or a Chinese concubine on his last visit to the physical plane.

In Bernstein's opinion, one could only take one of two points of view in regard to the strange case of Bridey Murphy. One might conclude that the whole thing had been a hoax without a motive. This conclusion would hold that Mrs. Simmons was not the "normal young gal" she seemed to be, but actually a frustrated actress who proved to be a consummate performer in her interpretation of a script dreamed up by Morey Bernstein "because he likes to fool people."

If one were not to accept that particular hypothesis, Bernstein said, then the public must admit that the experiment may have opened a hidden door for just a second, and that, without fully understanding what had been seen, it had been an exciting glimpse of immortality.

Doubleday released Morey Bernstein's *The Search for Bridey Murphy* in 1956. Bernstein claimed that he had invested $10,000 in his exploration of Bridey's assertion of a physical existence and that he did not hope to earn that much in royalties from sales of the book. Furthermore, the businessman stated, he did not care if his expenditures were met or not. He had, he hoped, opened up an important facet of man's existence for further exploration.

Skeptics and serious investigators alike were interested in testing Bernstein's thesis that Bridey Murphy had given America an "exciting glimpse of immortality."

In mid-January 1956, the *Chicago Daily News* sent its London representative on a three-day safari into Ireland. He was assigned to check out Cork, Dublin, and Belfast and uncover any evidence which might serve as verification for the Bridey Murphy claims. With only one day for each city, it is not surprising that the newsman reported that he could find nothing of significance.

In February, the *Denver Post* sent William Barker, the man who first reported the story of the search for Bridey Murphy, to conduct a thorough investigation of the enigma. Barker felt that certain strong points had already been established by Irish investigators and had been detailed in Bernstein's book.

Bridey (Irish spelling of the name is Bridie) had said that her father-in-law, John MacCarthy, had been a barrister (lawyer) in Cork. A lawyer in Dublin had written the book publishers on September 30, 1954, and informed them that there was a John MacCarthy from Cork, a Roman Catholic educated at Clongowes School, listed in the Registry of Kings Inn.

Bridey had mentioned a "greengrocer," John Carrigan, with whom she had traded in Belfast. A Belfast librarian, in a letter dated May 19, 1955, had attested to the fact that there had been a man of that name and trade at 90 Northumberland during the time in which the personality of Bridey Murphy had claimed to have lived there.

The librarian, a Mr. John Bebbington, had also verified the personality's statement that there had been a William Farr who had sold foodstuffs during this same period.

One of the most significant bits of information had to do with a place that Bridey Murphy had called Mourne. Such a place was not shown on any modern maps of Ireland, but its existence was substantiated through the British Information Service.

While entranced, Ruth Simmons had "remembered" that Catholics could teach at Queen's University, Belfast, even though it was a Protestant institution. American investigators had made a hasty prejudgment when they learned of such a statement and had challenged the likelihood of such an interdenominational teaching arrangement. In Ireland, however, such a fact was common knowledge, and Bridey had scored another hit.

Barker conceded that any one of the items taken separately did not constitute proof of reincarnation. The newsman did feel, however, that all of the details combined did begin to add up to a most provocative case for the defense.

Then there were such things as Bridey knowing about the old Irish custom of dancing at weddings and putting money in the bride's pockets. There was also her familiarity with the currency of that period, the crops of the region, the contemporary musical pieces, and the folklore of the area.

When Barker dined with a hotel owner who was interested in the "search," the newsman questioned Bridey's referring to certain food being prepared in "flats."

"Flats" wasn't a word we knew in that context, Barker told his host, Kenneth Besson. Besson waved a waiter to their table and asked him to bring some flats. When the waiter returned, Barker saw that flats were like platters, far as he could see. It was a perfectly normal term there, Besson said.

Several scholars had felt that Bridey had committed a gross error when she mentioned the custom of kissing the Blarney stone.

The Blarney superstition was a comparatively late-nineteenth-century notion, Dermot Foley, the Cork city librarian told Barker.

Later Foley told the reporter that he owed Bridey an apology. T. Crofton Cronker, in his *Researches in the South of Ireland, 1824,* mentions the custom of kissing the Blarney stone as early as 1820.

But Bridey Murphy did not always score. Numerous Irish historians and scholars felt that she must have been more Scottish than Irish. They were especially firm about the name Duncan, which she had given for that of her father and her brother.

"I wonder if she might have been tryin' to say Dunnock instead of Duncan," speculated John Collins, described as a "walking history book" of Irish customs.

On Barker's long flight home to Denver, he tried to organize his conclusions. Later, he published the findings of his own private search for Bridey Murphy in the *Post*.

On the debit side, Bridey had been wrong about most of her people, even about alleged facts in her own life. Barker had been unable to find complete birth data on either Bridey or her kin. The personality had used the word "barrister" with a frequency that amazed educated Irishmen. And Bridey had shocked most Irishmen with her crude term "ditched" to describe her burial. Barker was told that the Irish are much too reverent toward the dead to employ such a brutal word.

The personality, speaking through Mrs. Simmons, had demonstrated little knowledge of Ireland's history from 1800 to the 1860's. Bridey and Brian's honeymoon route had become hopelessly untraceable and confused with the trip she had made to Antrim as a child of ten. The principal difficulty in accepting Bridey's story lay in the fact that so much of the testimony was untraceable and unverifiable.

On the credit side of Bridey Murphy's ledger were all the many things which she had been right about, even though the scholars and the authorities at first stated that she was wrong.

There was the matter of the iron bed which she had scratched with her fingernails. Certain authorities discredited this statement on the grounds that iron beds had not yet been introduced into Ireland during the period in which Bridey had claimed to live. The *Encyclopaedia Britannica,* however, states that iron beds did appear in Bridey's era and were advertised as being "free from the insects which sometimes infected wooden bedsteads."

Extremely convincing is Bridey's vocabulary. If the whole thing were nothing other than an elaborate hoax, Ruth Simmons must rate as one of the most brilliant character actresses of all time. One of the most difficult things to attain in achieving a convincing characterization is the speech pattern of the person being mimed. Our speech patterns are as distinctive as our fingerprints. The personality of Bridey Murphy never faltered in her almost poetic speech, and, of the hundreds of words of jargon and colloquial phrases which she uttered, nearly all were found to be just right for the time in which she claimed to have lived. The songs which Bridey sang, her graphic word pictures of wake and marriage customs were all acclaimed by Irish folklorists as being accurate.

Her grim reference to the "black something" which took the life of her baby brother probably referred to famine or disease. The Irish use of "black" in this manner means "malignant" and would have nothing to do with the actual color of the pestilence.

Barker found that Bridey had bested the authorities on several occasions. Bridey's claims to have eaten muffins as a child, to have obtained books from a lending library in Belfast, to have known about the Blarney stone were, at first, judged to be out of proper time context. Later, her challengers actually uncovered historical substantiation for the statements made by Bridey through Ruth Simmons.

What did he think about the whole Bridey business? Barker wrote. It was no fraud, he said, whatever it was. And it wasn't telepathy.

Certain researchers of psychic phenomena have disagreed with this analysis. While agreeing that the Bridey Murphy case is not a consciously contrived fraud, many investigators will not rule out the role that telepathy or some other extrasensory ability may have played in the "memory" of the Irish housewife.

First of all, one must concede that certain items could have been "remembered" by the Colorado housewife via normal means and could have been dug out of her subconscious by the hypnotic trance induced by Morey Bernstein. "Mrs. S." could have had several acquaintances throughout her childhood who were familiar with Ireland and who may have each imparted a bit of the memory of "Bridey Murphy."

Many skeptical researchers tried to apply the phenomenon of cryptomnesia to Ruth Simmons (later disclosed to be Mrs. Virginia Tighe), who was adopted in infancy by her mother's sister, a woman with the typical mixed heritage of the average American. Cryptomnesia holds that a child might somehow have known a person who relayed the information which he later seemed to remember about a previous life. The child would have forgotten both the source of his "memory" and the fact that he had ever obtained it, although he would remember the information so that he might dramatically present it as recalled from a past incarnation. The attempts to discredit Bridey Murphy as a manifestation of cryptomnesia fail in the estimation of researchers C. J. Ducasse and Ian Stevenson. In Stevenson's estimation, the critics of the Bridey Murphy case provided only suppositions of possible sources of information, not evidence that these had been the sources.

It cannot be denied that Bridey possessed a knowledge of nineteenth-century Ireland which contained a number of items of information which were unfamiliar even to authorities and historians. Such details, when checked after elaborate research, were found to be correct in Bridey's favor.

When the reader finds himself up against these annoying "hits" that cannot be undermined by the most penetrating analysis, he also finds himself forced to admit that "Mrs. S.," alias Bridey Murphy, either acquired the information paranormally (i.e., through extrasensory means) or by reliving the memory of a past life.

CHAPTER ELEVEN:
EAST IS EAST
AND WEST IS WEST

Even though many of the great minds who have shaped the intellectual and religious climate of the West held firm beliefs in reincarnation (i.e., Plato, St. Augustine, St. Clement, St. Jerome), historically, at least since the fourth century A.D., ecclesiastical Christian dogmatists have spoken out against the doctrine of rebirth. Only a slightly more liberal attitude exists today, and American parents would certainly not encourage a kindergartener to come forward with alleged memories of a prior existence. Doctor, priest, and PTA would descend upon the unfortunate child with the fervor of Grand Inquisitors.

Dr. Ian Stevenson, who has done a great deal of investigation into situations wherein individuals have claimed to recall former lives, has amassed more than 600 cases suggestive of reincarnation. The researcher, presently of the Department of Neurology and Psychiatry of the University of Virginia, has found these cases distributed all over the globe, among peoples of widely varying cultural patterns, and among societies where the religious dogmas sternly preach against a belief in reincarnation.

As the reader progresses into his study of this subject, he will note, as did Dr. Stevenson, that cases suggestive of reincarnation all have certain factors in com-

mon which seem completely unrelated to and independent of the percipient's cultural environment.
Whether the case should occur in India, England, or
the United States, certain basic features remain constant:

A small child, two to four years of age, begins to
protest to his parents or brothers and sisters that he
wishes to return to his former home, wife, children, or
possessions. The child graphically describes his former
life and generally expresses a dissatisfaction with his inability to return to the geographical environment which
he was forced to leave at the event of his death.

A point to be stressed is that even though the majority of Eastern cultures (Indian, Ceylonese, Bur-
mese) maintain a belief in reincarnation as a part of
their religious faiths, young children are definitely not
encouraged to "remember" past lives. On the contrary,
a child who claims such memories will generally be
strongly admonished to forget the whole thing. In the
cases which follow, we will see that the parents often
feel no compunction in administering physical punishment when their offspring persist in claiming memories
of a prior existence.

In spite of threats of punishment and a chorus of
mockery from his siblings, we see that the child persists in his allegations. He experiences a strong pull
back toward the life that has recently terminated, and
he continues to beg his present parents to allow him to
return to the community where he lived in his previous
incarnation.

If the child continues in his persistence and in his
recall of intimate details of another existence, the parents may reluctantly begin to make inquiries about the
accuracy of the story which their child babbles. In many
cases, the investigation will not occur until several years

after the child has begun to speak of his memories. In each of the cases which we shall examine, we shall see that this delay in investigation speaks very convincingly against any charge of conspiracy or fraud on the part of the parents. In many of the stories presented in this book, the parents have reacted with emotions and attitudes ranging from disinterest to violent anger when their child persisted in his claims of a previous incarnation. All of the parents were publicity shy and had no desire to put their offspring on display for monetary gain.

If the parents do begin some attempts at verification and if some positive results are obtained, members of the two families involved may visit each other for the purpose of interrogating the child. He may be asked if he remembers persons, objects, past incidents, and personal experiences of his alleged previous existence. If the child scores an impressive series of hits, his story will create a great deal of attention in the communities involved and, in most cases, local newspapers will be alerted to the event.

In recent years, the Indian Society for Psychical Research has sent investigators to document cases suggestive of reincarnation, but it is impossible to determine how many dramatic cases have never been researched due to angry and frustrated parents suppressing a child's memories with threats and demonstrations of physical punishment. Even though the religions of India may include reincarnation in their doctrines, I feel we must reemphasize the fact that no Indian mother crouches over her child's cradle at night and encourages him to recall a past life.

I think another most impressive point in the cases which we shall examine is the early age at which the child begins to graphically describe a former life. It would seem to be beyond belief that a two-year-old boy could speak so eloquently in protest of his murder at the hands of a debtor, solely from the aspect of the mechanics of speech and articulation, let alone the manifestation of reincarnation.

In each of the following cases, the young child truly seems to be an "old soul," much advanced beyond his peer group in proficiency of speech, application of intellect, and sociability. Imagine the reaction of the various widows, whom we shall meet in these chapters, when they hear intimate details of their marriage relationship from the lips of two-year-old boys, who continue to speak frankly of matters which only their husbands would know.

Truly, fraud would seem to be out of the question in such cases. No two-year-old is capable of being coached to perpetrate such elaborate hoaxes. No child's brain is capable of memorizing countless details of the lives of obscure men and women who died in remote and desolate villages. And what motive would a parent have to precipitate such a hoax? What would justify the countless hours necessary to coach a two-year-old to recite the details of the life of a housewife of a butcher in a nearby village? The Indian newspapers do not offer a reward for the year's best case suggestive of reincarnation.

No, something is at work here. Whether it be extrasensory perception, possession by a discarnate soul, or reincarnation will be judged according to the personal bias of each reader. All that I shall present are the documented facts.

"DON'T CALL ME ISMAIL"

The young boy looked at his father, lying on the bed beside him, and said, "I am tired of living here. I want to go back to my house and children."

Mehemet Altinklish listened to these strange notions coming from the mouth of his son Ismail—a mere child of eighteen months! "What did you say, Ismail?" he asked.

"Don't call me Ismail," the boy insisted. "I am Abeit."

Upon being questioned by his father, the boy insisted that he was the reincarnation of Abeit Suzulmus, a prosperous market gardener who had been murdered shortly before Ismail's birth.

Abeit, who lived in the Bahchehe section of the Midik District of Adana, Turkey, had gardens of sufficient size that it was necessary for him to hire laborers. Three such laborers came to him looking for work one day and he employed them. For unknown reasons, they lured Abeit into his stable and there beat him to death with an iron bar.

The killers then went to the house and slaughtered Abeit's second wife, Sahida, and two of their children. The murders took place on January 31, 1956.

A week later the killers were caught. They were tried and convicted. Two were hanged; the other died in prison.

A few short months after the murders, Ismail was born in another section of the Midik District, about three-quarters of a mile from Abeit's gardens. From the time he was a year and a half old, the boy insisted that he was Abeit Suzulmus, exhibiting a very strong identification with the murdered man. So strong was this identification that he continually begged his parents to let him visit Abeit's home.

When he reached the age of three, his parents finally agreed to such a trip.

Leading a party of twelve, young Ismail traversed the distance between the homes unaided and without error, even though several members of the party deliberately tried to lead him astray. As young as he was and never having wandered very far from his present home, it is highly unlikely that Ismail could have made the complicated journey without some prior knowledge or familiarity with the route. Ismail claimed to have attained this familiarity from his previous life.

When the group reached the house, Ismail identified the members of Abeit's family from a crowd of about thirty persons, calling them by name and embracing them as he did so. He referred to them as Hatice, "my first wife"; Gulsarin, "my daughter"; Hikmat, "my daughter"; and Zaki, "my son."

During this first visit, the boy led the party to the two-room stable saying, "Let me show you where I was murdered," and he pointed to the exact spot. Abeit-Ismail also commented that some of the equipment and furnishings in the stable had been removed since his death.

In another revelation of the life of Abeit, Ismail stated that, at one time during his life, Abeit loaned money to Abdul, but they did not know the amount of the loan or whether it had ever been repaid. Abdul confirmed the fact that he still owed money to the Suzulmus family.

The Adana press carried an incident occurring between Ismail and an ice-cream vendor who seldom visited the area of Ismail's home. According to the newspaper, Ismail confronted the vendor, a man called Mehemet, and asked if he recognized him. When the vendor replied in the negative, Ismail said, "You have forgotten me. I am Abeit. You did not sell ice cream before, but watermelons and vegetables."

The vendor said that this was true. Ismail went on to tell the vendor about a time when he, Abeit, had performed the circumcision ceremony for him. When they parted, the vendor was thoroughly convinced that he had met Abeit in a new life.

Another time, a cowherd named Mezit who was employed by the Suzulmus family was leading a cow past the Altinklish home. Ismail recognized Mezit, calling him by name and inquiring whether the cow was his (Abeit's) "yellow girl."

So real are the memory patterns of Abeit to Ismail that he often speaks of his former life in the present tense, such as, "I have a house and family," or "Here is my grave." He has begged many times to be allowed to go and live with his (the Suzulmus) family, although this has been generally discouraged. Even then, he takes them sweets, despite the fact that his family cannot afford it. Strange sacrifices for a child so young.

Ismail's obsession with Abeit has even penetrated his sleep. Often he has been heard crying out, "Gulsarin! Gulsarin!" and awakened showing great emotion. It is hard to imagine that anything other than deeply seeded factual experiences could bring on such a display of concern, particularly when the subject is sleeping.

Professor H. N. Banerjee, editor of the *Journal of Parapsychology,* interviewed the boy and all concerned extensively, and concluded that it seemed more certain than usual that this particular case had not arisen through any desire to defraud. Banerjee noted that the family had not sought any publicity for the case and had, in fact, resisted for a year and a half the boy's demands to go to Abeit Suzulmus' home. When Banerjee and the press arrived on the scene, the family of Ismail were most reluctant to cooperate. Reports of the case had not even reached the outside world until three years after Ismail had first visited Abeit's home.

Banerjee also reported that ill feelings had arisen between the two families involved. It would seem most unlikely that a fraud could be so ingeniously perpetrated when those involved are not on speaking terms with one another.

THE THIRD TIME AROUND

Those who truly believe in the reality of reincarnation feel that the case of Swarnlata Mishra adds heavy ammunition to their cause. Swarnlata, the daughter of no less a personage than the Vice-Chancellor of Saugor University and former Home Minister of Madya Pradesh, India, claimed verifiable memories of two lives when she was but ten years old.

"My name is Biya," the small girl told her family. "I was born about 1900. I had four brothers and two sisters. One of my younger brothers was Babu."

"Babu," she later related, was her pet name for her younger brother, Hari Prasad Pathak, and was what she had always called him when they were at home.

Hari heard of the strange claims of the ten-year-old girl and decided to make a trip to the Mishra home in order that he might convince himself of their validity. His sister Biya had been dead for almost twenty years! He made the journey to Chhatarpur in April 1959.

Upon meeting the young girl, Hari questioned her regarding details of their childhood home, household articles, and many other family characteristics. As Hari stood in awe, the little girl told him not only of the location of their former home, but its size, color, and shape as well. She recalled how their old home had been furnished inside, and she told him of many incidents that had happened decades before.

Chintamani Pandey, Biya's husband, and Murli Pandey, her son, also heard of Swarnlata's claims. They, too, were curious about this girl who said that she had lived a past life as mother of their family; so they traveled from Katni to Chhatarpur to see her.

Immediately Swarnlata recognized them both, expressing joy and asking of their well-being. When Chintamani produced an old group photo, she looked at it and smiled. "This is you, here, but you were much younger then."

Swarnlata was invited to the Pathak house for a visit, whereupon she was presented with some more group photographs, many of them quite old. From these, she easily identified her mother and father as well as two other brothers and an old servant.

Swarnlata's father, D. P. Mishra, recalls a family auto trip which they took when his daughter was about four years of age. As the car neared Katni (the childhood home of Biya), the child became very excited and asked the driver, "Take me to the house where I was born."

Little notice was taken of her remark until later. When they stopped at a roadside stand for tea, Swarnlata said, "We could take tea at my old house in Katni."

Her father dismissed her mutterings as nothing but childish babble and turned his attentions back to the trip.

The woman Biya died in 1939.

But there was no long time gap between Biya and Swarnlata. The ten-year-old daughter of a government official was to recall yet another life.

She told her parents that, that same year when Biya died, she was reborn into a Brahmin family at Silhatte in Assam state. In this life, her name was Kamlesh and her parents' names were Ramesh and Shashimata. They were people of means, for Kamlesh was taken to school each day in her own private automobile.

But the good life was not to last for her. One day, when she was nine years old, the car crashed into a tree, fatally injuring her. She died in a hospital shortly after the accident.

Her father, D. P. Mishra, says that as early as the age of four, Swarnlata sang Assamese folk songs and performed Assamese tribal dances. Investigation has shown both the dances and the songs to be quite authentic, indeed strange in view of the fact that Swarnlata had never been outside the geographical boundaries of Madya Pradesh, nor, as her father confirms, had she ever come in contact with any Assamese.

H. P. Pastore, a former president of the Municipal Board of Chhatarpur, interviewed the girl, checking and verifying all other data, and came to the following conclusion: ". . . It is quite evident that what she claims to recall actually are memories of former lives."

THE EXECUTIONER LEFT HIS MARK

"I'm worried about our son," said Mrs. Hami to her husband. "He seems as if he were in another world. All he does all day long is wander around the house talking to himself."

"But it's common for young children to go around babbling." H. A. Tileratne Hami had no fears for his child. The woman's worries were obviously unfounded.

But the mother was not to pass it off that easily. For days she followed the two year old around the house, listening to him. Gradually, in bits and pieces, she picked up the gist of what he was saying.

Wijeratne was talking about another life! He muttered to himself about his arm being deformed because he had murdered his wife in his former life. The laws of Karma were doing their justice.

Mrs. Hami immediately recalled a conversation which she had had earlier with her husband in which she remembered his commenting that there were marked similarities between his son, Wijeratne, and his deceased brother, Ratran Hami. Even later when her husband had said, "This is my brother come back," she had not paid much attention to it. Now she began to wonder.

She told her husband what the boy had said concerning the murder of his "wife," and she asked him questions about Ratran Hami, a subject hitherto unmentioned in the household. H. A. Tileratne had always been vague in reference to his brother. Now, with the question put to him and the overwhelming evidence reiterated by his son, he told her the story.

Tileratne Hami and his brother, Ratran Hami, had been farmers in the village of Uggalkaltota at the time. Tileratne was some fifteen years the elder, but it was Ratran who got married first. On October 14, 1927, Ratran, and his wife, Podi Menike, had come to some disagreement. As a result of the argument, the bride refused to leave her parents' home and go with Ratran to his village. This angered Ratran to the extent that he drew forth his *kris* and assaulted the disobedient wife, subsequently killing her.

The murderous bridegroom was tried, convicted, and sentenced to hang. When the sentence of the court had been pronounced, Tileratne went to his brother and asked him if there were anything he could do.

Ratran replied, "I am not afraid. I know that I will have to die. I am only worried about you. Don't sorrow, my brother. I will return."

In July 1928, Ratran was executed.

In August 1961, Dr. Ian Stevenson and Francis Story interviewed Wijeratne with members of his family and were able to throw a little more light on the "why" of the case. Marriages in Ceylon are accomplished in two stages. When a marriage is agreed upon, usually by the parents of the families involved, a legal contract is drawn up. A delay may then occur before the formal wedding feast and the domestic union and consummation of the marriage. During the interval between legal marriage and wedding feast it is not uncommon for the bride to continue to live at her parents' home, but she must remain in readiness to depart with her husband when he calls for her. Such was the case of Ratran and Podi Menike. The legal ceremony had taken place, but the final ones were yet to come.

Wijeratne relates that he (Ratran-Wijeratne) feared that his wife had become infatuated with another man, who had persuaded her not to go through with her marriage to Ratran. When it came time for the final step of the marriage, Ratran went to his wife's house to get her. She refused.

The bridegroom pleaded with her, but when Podi would not be swayed, he walked the five miles back to his own home. There he got out his knife and sharpened it. He returned to the house of Podi Menike and once again begged her to return with him to consummate their marriage.

Again Podi refused, and then Ratran saw that his beloved was in the company of his rival. Being thus angered, Ratran fell upon the wayward wife and ended her infidelity—and her life.

Wijeratne-Ratran says he definitely remembers the gallows and the sensations he underwent as the trap was sprung. It seemed as though he were dropping into a pit of fire. After that he forgot everything until he was two years old and realized that he had been reborn as his brother's son.

When he talks of the murder, Wijeratne states, "I had an unbearable temper at the time. I did not think of the punishment I would get." He continues, "But I do not think that I did wrong. If I were again faced with the situation of a disobedient wife, I think I would act as before."

How did a boy of two acquire such an enormous amount of exacting information about a past life and a past crime when, in fact, his mother had never known of the incident and his father had never mentioned his uncle's execution around the house? Ariyaratne, Wijeratne's older brother by seven years, verifies the fact that his father had never spoken of Ratran and that Wijeratne began to narrate the story in great detail when he was no more than two and a half years old!

Wijeratne has since given up spontaneously speaking of the subject, but will talk about it freely whenever it is mentioned.

In Volume XXVI, *Proceedings of the American Society for Psychical Research,* September 1966 ("Twenty Cases Suggestive of Reincarnation"), Dr. Ian Stevenson concludes his investigation by commenting on Wijeratne's statement that, as Ratran Hami, he had killed Podi Menike and, in similar circumstances, he would not hesitate to kill her again. The researcher points out that Ratran Hami pleaded innocent at his trial. Stevenson seems inclined to believe that this difference supports the reincarnation hypothesis as opposed to the theory that Wijeratne obtained his information through extrasensory perception from his parents or, conceivably, from the court records. Investigator Stevenson feels that if Wijeratne had acquired his information from these sources, he would have adhered to the plea of "not guilty."

CHAPTER TWELVE:
KARMA:
THE DIVINE JUSTICE

Author Berry Benson once phrased the dogma of reincarnation in the analogy of a small boy who enters school and is placed by his teacher in the lowest class and charged with learning these lessons: Thou shalt not kill. Thou shalt do no hurt to any living thing. Thou shalt not steal.

So the little boy grew into a man. He did not kill, but he became cruel and he stole. At the end of the day "when his beard was gray; when the night had come," the teacher noted that although the student had not killed, he had failed to learn his other lessons. "Come back again tomorrow," the teacher told him.

When the new day dawned, the pupil returned to school and was placed in a higher class because he had accomplished one lesson. Then the teacher gave him these lessons to learn: Thou shalt do no hurt to any living thing. Thou shalt not cheat. Thou shalt not steal.

Again the boy grew into a man. He was careful to do no hurt to any living thing, and he tried not to be cruel. But he stole from his neighbors and he cheated to accomplish his own ends. At the end of the day, "when his beard was gray; when the night had come," the teacher recognized the fact that the student had learned to be merciful, but he had failed to accomplish the other lessons. Once again, the student was told to return on the morrow.

So it may be with man. Jesus Christ admonished man to be perfect even as God is perfect. Such perfection cannot be achieved in a single lifetime. It would seem more just to allow a man to return again and again, until all the "lessons" have been learned, before his soul stands to judgment and is examined as to whether it is worthy of attaining eternal life in the God Consciousness or should be shut away from God's grace.

"Even the best men are not, when they die, in such a state of intellectual and mortal perfection as would fit them to enter heaven immediately," commented John M. Ellis McTaggart in *Some Dogmas of Religion*. McTaggart speculates that the man who dies after acquiring knowledge might enter his new life deprived of that particular bit of knowledge, ". . . but not deprived of the increased strength and delicacy of mind which he gained in acquiring the knowledge. . . . So a man may carry over into his next life the disposition and tendencies which he has gained by the moral contests of this life, and the value of those experiences will not have been destroyed by the death which has destroyed the memory of them."

If you have absorbed the understanding that God is love; that as you sow, so shall you reap; that as you plant, so gather you in; you will know that there is no punishment. You are not punished for the deeds you have committed, either in this life, or in the life to come. They are shown to you, clear and defined, and then you are left free to work out the mistakes of the past. It is not punishment visited upon you; it is but the natural working of God's law; it is but cause and effect in operation. It is Karma.

The cycle of rebirth is discussed, evaluated, and

accepted in the most ancient texts of all cultures. The *Hermes Trismegistus,* which set forth the esoteric doctrines of the ancient Egyptian priesthood, recognizes the reincarnation of "impious souls" and the achievement of pious souls when they know God and become "all intelligence." It decrees against transmigration, the belief that the soul of men may enter into animals. "Divine law preserves the human soul from such infamy," state the Hermetic books.

The *Bhagavad-Gita,* holy text of the Hindus, observes:

As the dweller in the body experienceth childhood, youth, old age, so passeth he on to another body; the steadfast one grieveth not thereat. . . .

He who regardeth himself as a slayer, or he who thinketh he is slain, both of them are ignorant. He slayeth not, nor is he slain.

He is not born, nor does he die; nor having been, ceaseth he any more to be; unborn, perpetual, eternal and ancient, he is not slain when the body is slaughtered.

As a man, casting off worn-out garments, taketh new ones, so the dweller in the body, casting off worn-out bodies, entereth into others that are new. . . .

For certain is death for the born, and certain is birth for the dead; therefore over the inevitable thou shouldst not grieve.

Our Judeo-Christian heritage is hardly devoid of the doctrine of reincarnation.

In his *Lux Orientalis,* Joseph Glanvil states that man's preexistence was a philosophy commonly held by the Jews; this is illustrated by the disciples' ready questioning of Jesus when they asked: "Master, was it for this man's sin or his father's that he was born blind?" If the disciples had not believed that the blind man had lived another life in which he might have sinned, Glanvil argues, the question would have been senseless and impertinent.

When Christ asked his disciples who men said He was, they answered that some said John the Baptist, others Elias, others Jeremiah or one of the prophets. Glanvil reasons that such a response on the part of the disciples demonstrates their belief in metempsychosis and preexistence. "These, one would think, were very proper occasions for our Savior to have rectified His mistaken followers had their supposition been an error. . . ."

Andre Pezzani takes issue with the Christian doctrine of man's original sin in *The Plurality of the Soul's Existence:* "Original sin does not account for the particular fate of individuals, as it is the same for all. . . ." Once man accepts the theory of preexistence, Pezzani holds, ". . . a glorious light is thrown on the dogma of sin, for it becomes the result of personal faults from which the guilty soul must be purified. Pre-existence, once admitted as regards the past, logically implies a succession of future existences for all souls that have not yet attained to the goal, and that have imperfections and defilements from which to be cleansed. In order to enter the *circle of happiness* and leave the *circle of wanderings,* one must be pure."

In the opinion of Eva Gore-Booth, such is the role that Christ assumes in God's Great Plan—to offer man release from the cycle of rebirth. Christ came to offer eternal life to all men ". . . a deliverance from reincarnation, from the life and death circle of this earthly living, not from any torments of a bodiless state, but simply from the body of this death." In *A Psychological and Poetic Approach to the Study of Christ in the Fourth Gospel,* she writes: "The idea of a succession of lives and deaths, following one another, for those who have not yet attained real life—are not yet Sons of God and children of the Resurrection—seems to illuminate, in a curious way, some of Christ's most profound and seemingly paradoxical teaching on the destiny and the hope, the life or death of the human psyche."

Origen (185 A.D. to 254 A.D.) devoted his life to the preservation of the original gospels. A prolific Christian writer, Origen maintained a relationship between faith and knowledge and explained the sinfulness of all men by the doctrine of the preexistence of all souls.

"Is it not rational that souls should be introduced into bodies in accordance with their merits and previous deeds, and that those who have used their bodies in doing the utmost possible good should have a right to bodies endowed with qualities superior to the bodies of others?" he asked in *Contra Celsum*. "The soul, which is immaterial and invisible in its nature, exists in no material place without having a body suited to the nature of that place; accordingly, it at one time puts off one body, which is necessary before, but which is no longer adequate in its changed state, and it exchanges it for a second."

In the *De Principiis,* Origen stated that ". . . every soul . . . comes into this world strengthened by the victories or weakened by the defeats of its previous life. Its place in this world as a vessel appointed to honor or dishonor is determined by its previous merits or demerits. . . . I am indeed of the opinion that as the end and consummation of the saints will be in those [ages] which are not seen and are eternal, we must conclude that rational creatures had also a similar beginning. . . . And if this is so, then there has been a descent from a higher to a lower condition, on the part not only of those souls who have deserved the change . . . but also on that of those who, in order to serve the whole world, were brought down from those higher and invisible spheres to these lower and visible ones. . . . The hope of freedom is entertained by the whole of creation—of being liberated from the corruption of slavery—when the sons of God, who either fell away or were scattered abroad shall be gathered into one, and when they shall have fulfilled their duties in this world."

At the Council of Nicaea in 325 A.D., Origenism was excluded from the doctrines of the Church and fifteen anathemas were proposed against Origen. The Origenists had lost by only one vote, but, as stated by Head and Cranston in *Reincarnation, An East-West Anthology*, ". . . Catholic scholars are beginning to disclaim that the Roman Church took any part in the anathemas against Origen. . . . However, one disastrous result of the mistakes still persists; namely, the exclusion from the Christian creed of the teaching of the pre-existence of the soul, and, by implication, reincarnation."

It seems now that once again man is willing to consider that it is his transcendental self, his basic essence, which has introduced him into life and has determined his particular individuality. Whatever earthly misery he may confront, the man who has come to recognize the transcendental spark within himself will see that such suffering is for his own transcendental advantage. Those who have glimpsed a bit of the transcendental self have come to know that man is his own heir, that what man has gained morally and intellectually remains with him.

"A man has a soul, and it passes from life to life,

as a traveler from inn to inn, till at length it is ended in heaven," H. Fielding Hall wrote in *The Soul of a People*. "But not till he has attained heaven in his heart will he attain heaven in reality."

The ethics of Karma were delineated by Gina Cerminara in *Many Mansions*. In Chapter XXIV, "A Philosophy to Live By," Dr. Cerminara, a trained psychologist, presents the essence of the wisdom which she received from an extensive study of the Edgar Cayce readings while residing at Virginia Beach.

In outline form this pattern seems to be as follows:

God exists.
Every soul is a portion of God.
    (You *are* a soul; you inhabit a body.)
Life is purposeful.
Life is continuous.
All human life operates under law.
    (Karma; reincarnation)
Love fulfills that law.
The will of man creates his destiny.
The mind of man has formative power.
The answer to all problems is within the Self.

In accordance with the above postulates, man is enjoined as follows:

Realize first your relationship to the Creative
    Forces of the Universe, or God.
Formulate your ideals and purposes in life.
Strive to achieve those ideals.
Be active.
Be patient.
Be joyous.

Leave the results to God.
Do not seek to evade any problem.
Be a channel of good to other people.

E. D. Walker portrayed the doctrine of reincarnation as uniting all the family of man into a universal brotherhood. Reincarnation ". . . promotes the solidarity of mankind by destroying the barriers that conceit and circumstances have raised between individuals, groups, nations, and races. There are no special gifts . . . successes are the laborious result of long merit . . . failures proceed from negligence. The upward road to . . . spiritual perfection is always at our feet. . . . The downward way to sensual wreckage is but the other direction of the same way. We cannot despise those who are tending down, for who knows but we have journeyed that way ourselves? It is impossible for us to scramble up alone, for our destiny is included in that of humanity, and only by helping others along can we ascend ourselves."

A fitting attitudinal approach to a study of the claimed memories of former lives might be found in the personal creed of Friedrich Nietzsche: "Live so that thou mayest desire to live again—that is thy duty; for in any case, thou wilt live again!"

Francie, the principal channel for the Starbirth Foundation of Scottsdale, Arizona, dealt with the divine justice of Karma in her *Reflections from an Angel's Eye:*

In the realm of Eternity where Time is nonexistent, there dwells the Hierarchy. While patiently watching the plight of its seedlings on Earth, the Heavenly Host could see that the fallen Souls and humankind were not spiritually evolving. If man continued on this errant path, he would never become incorporated into his Soul and enter the Hierarchal Realm.

The Hierarchy had hoped that when Divine Justice had been established on the Earth plane—wherein mankind would reap an exact measure of what he sowed—he would learn from such experiences and thereby raise his vibrations to the Hierarchal Realm. He would come to realize that to sow that which was good for others, might enable him to reap good for himself. But all on Earth continued to be shackled to the endless treadmill of thwarting the growth of his fellowman and thereby preventing his own advancement.

Therefore, a Divine Plan was devised by the Hierarchy to aid mankind in becoming aware of the heritage that could be his. If mankind could realize the form of justice that was established on Earth for the purpose of raising his vibrations and those of his Soul, he would then live his life differently, thus gaining in awareness so that he might escape this planet of learning. This Divine Plan would give mankind an awareness of its purpose, teach him of the laws of Karma, and warn him of the full consequences that would befall him if he defied such a system. As a wise parent gives love or punishment to a child to instruct him, so must mankind realize that such a Pavlovian method consisting of reward or punishment exists on Earth.

The Hierarchy knew well the reaction of man if they would intervene and approach mankind by opening the dimension to the world of higher vibrations. If they would tell all that must be done to escape the pains and lessons to be learned on Earth so as to ascend to their world, they realized they would not be teaching mankind but would only cause blind and fear-filled obedience. Thus nothing could be learned, for man would then be controlled. With such a denial of freedom mankind would be as a robot reacting through blind obedience.

The Hierarchy realized that they must incarnate in flesh-forms, as well as enter into the minds of man so as to act within the established order to effect a change on Earth. This, they knew, was the only way that mankind could gain knowledge and thereby raise his vibrations as well as those of his Soul and leave this realm of lower vibrations.

Many members of the Hierarchy incarnated on Earth to teach the laws of Divine Justice long since established, and to instruct mankind in the ways in which to raise his vibrations. They helped make man aware of his true cosmic heritage. Many of these incarnated Hierarchal entities realized that their flesh-forms would be attacked and undergo many torments. They knew that they would suffer greatly, and in some cases, even be destroyed for what would be considered radical teachings. They also understood that their Soul could not be harmed, though their flesh be destroyed. They were well aware that they would continue to incarnate as they taught mankind, generation after generation. They could perceive that all things which occurred were positive, for they could view the total picture and know all that would be gained.

Many of our prophets, leaders of ancient religions, and venerable philosophers who helped raise the consciousness of the masses were members of the incarnated Hierarchy. Those whose bodies were destroyed while performing their Earthly mission absorbed many of the Karmic misdeeds which had been sowed by mankind. This is the explanation of the oft-repeated phrase mentioned in the Christian Bible that

Jesus Christ died for our sins. His positive act absorbed much Karma which was due mankind on Earth.

The prophets also awakened mankind to the eventual and final reward of everlasting happiness that might be his if he lived to aid others, giving off positive vibrations. In the gaining of knowledge from all he experienced man would thereby elevate his vibrations and those of his Soul and escape this planet of learning.

Prophets and wisemen of old taught of the method of Karma that was established to aid mankind in gaining awareness and to raise its vibrations. What could be more fair than having everything you did to another returned to you? This is Divine Justice. Remember the phrases that tell of this justice: "Whatever is done unto the least of them will be done again unto you." "He who kills by the sword shall die by the sword." "That which you sow, you shall also reap."

We have been told that God alone, or the Karmic Law, metes out punishment when we were informed that revenge was not ours, but His. Revenge can only be taken by the Divine Justice of Karma, for in judging another, we have judged ourselves. "Judge not, lest ye be judged."

Misinterpreting the lessons, mankind has often set about to take it upon himself to punish all those he believes have disobeyed the laws established by the Hierarchy. In the *Bible,* a member of the Hierarchy who had incarnated as Elijah and who taught mankind before he returned to the Heavens in a "fiery chariot" (a glowing object) promised that he would descend to Earth once again before the coming of the Christ.

Hundreds of years later, Jesus was asked by a group he was teaching where Elijah was (since it had been foretold that the prophet would return before the

Christ). Jesus answered, "He has come already, and ye knew him not; for it is John the Baptist." Incarnating again and again the Hierarchy raised the consciousness of mankind.

Many times Jesus of Nazareth told his disciples that "they were not of this world, for if they were of this world, the world would love them." Jesus told them they were from another realm where they would return upon their death on Earth.

Several members of the Hierarchal Realm choosing to incarnate on Earth, purposely denied themselves the knowledge of their origin and their purpose in coming, so that they might enter as lambs before the slaughter and thereby more fully absorb the Karmic backlash due mankind.

How many times have we ourselves experienced the hideous thought that we have been singled out for punishment, and we have cried out during moments of intense pain, "Why me?" As their exists a veil from lifetime to lifetime in our Soul's incarnations on Earth, so was there chosen a veil of no foreknowledge by various members of the Hierarchy when they too incarnated on Earth.

CHAPTER THIRTEEN:
REINCARNATION—
OR A VOICE FROM BEYOND?

The voice spoke in a slow drawl. "Hope I'm not intrudin', but my name is Dave Dean. I'm a Kentuckian, a 'long hunter,' and the Shawnees scalped me!"

In the late fall of 1946 and on into 1947, author and psychic researcher Edmond P. Gibson attended a series of sittings with William H. Thatcher, a trance medium, in Grand Rapids, Michigan.

According to Gibson, the spirit personality which manifested did more toward proving survival and contributing to historical knowledge than Bridey Murphy dreamed of.

Speaking through Thatcher, the spirit voice told of being born in the 1760s, having lived for a time in Boonesboro, and being a member of George Rogers Clark's expedition to Kaskaskia. Many of the names which the medium relayed for Dave Dean were easily found and substantiated. Some of the facts and incidents which the spirit voice cited were at first thought to be totally incorrect. Extensive research in dusty old tomes proved that Dave Dean had been right. Although Dean was never too clear about his dates, he remembered details that seemed to be genuine memories of a physical existence in the frontier America of 1760 to 1800.

Even some of the most obscure items which Dave

Dean mentioned were later found to be historically correct. Attempts to trip the spirit of the frontiersman most often ended with a victory for Dave Dean.

Having Clark's memoirs of the expedition available, Gibson noted that on the march to Vincennes, the troops were frequently in water to their armpits. In his last sitting with the Thatcher séance circle, Gibson asked Dave what song the men sang as they marched to Vincennes.

The voice said they didn't do much marching, but were wading in water up to their waists most of the time.

Dave Dean cited "Lil Ol' Bolero" and "World Turned Upside Down" as two favorite songs of the men.

The investigators found that a song entitled "Lillibullero," written about 1766, had been very popular both among British soldiers and the frontiersmen. The original Spanish words were quickly corrupted on the frontier, and the lyrics were sung phonetically and with gusto by the backwoodsmen. It is easy to see how "Lillibullero" became "Lil Ol' Bolero" under such conditions of performance.

So it may have been with "World Turned Upside Down." In the *Journal of the American Society for Psychical Research* for July 1950, Dave Dean recalled as much as he could of the lyrics of this marching song:

> I've traveled far and I've traveled wide
> In every port and clime,
> [Here he says he forgets some of it.]
> I've drunk my lot, I've filled my shot
> In country and in town
> Till I got a wife.
> An' the world turned upside down.

They discovered that this march-time ballad was very popular among the British soldiers during the Revolution. Again, it is quite easy to see how homespun frontiersmen could have rearranged the lyrics in their version of "The World Turned Upside Down."

The communication of Dave Dean through the medium Thatcher fills forty single-spaced, typewritten pages. The entire transcript was sent to a nationally known historian, R. E. Banta, whose special interest in American history has been the Ohio River Valley.

"I not only 'care to look over' Dave Dean's communications, but I have read them through three times," Banta wrote the researchers. "This is one of the most interesting documents I've seen.

"Thatcher's subconscious is out, mainly. I have stowed away a great deal more information about the Ohio frontier than he can know exists and no one could call up any such volume as this, on short notice, out of my dormant cells.

". . . This thing could open up an entirely new field of historical research but it would surely catch hell from the 'union members' in the process!"

Although the possibility of the medium having extrasensory access to existing literary sources must be one of the hypotheses considered, many of the investigators favored the theory that an authentic communication from the dead had been received.

Might such communication from "beyond the grave" explain all cases of reincarnation?

Could it be that those who claim memories of past lives have become unwilling mediums and have been temporarily controlled by another personality?

This possession could last for but the duration of the period of mediumistic or hypnotic trance, or it might

last for several months, as in the case of Mary Roff–
Lurancy Vennum.

"Mother. I heard voices in my room last night. Voices
that called out 'Rancy, Rancy,' and it was as if I could
feel someone's breath on my face."

Such was the beginning of a marked change in the
life of Lurancy Vennum, a life that had been quite
normal and uneventful up until that morning in 1877.

Mary-Lurancy Vennum-Rancy—as she was called
by her family—was born on April 16, 1864, to James
J. Vennum and his wife Lurinda, near the town of
Watseka, Illinois. It was in her thirteenth year that the
strange occurrences began to take place.

On July 11, 1877, Lurancy began to have recurring
fits, sometimes several a day, oftentimes lapsing into
unconsciousness. Sometimes she became quite violent
and had to be restrained. At other times, she lay, almost corpselike, as if entombed in the ether of some
netherworld.

The trances, which lasted something over six months,
had varied effects on the young girl. At times she experienced pain and agony; on other occasions she
seemed to approach ecstasy. She spoke of heaven and
angels and of contact with the deceased.

Word of Lurancy's problem attracted more than a
passing interest from A. B. Roff, a highly respected
citizen in the community of Watseka. His daughter
Mary had undergone similar fits years earlier and had
subsequently died from one of them.

Because of his past experience, Mr. Roff sympathized
greatly with the Vennums and was finally able to persuade Mr. Vennum to allow him and an acquaintance,
Dr. E. W. Stevens, to come to the Vennum home to observe Lurancy. Dr. Stevens was a Wisconsin physician

and prominent psychical researcher. He was familiar with the case of Roff's daughter Mary, and hence greatly interested in another case so close, bearing such similarities.

When Roff and Stevens arrived at the Vennum residence on January 31, 1878, Lurancy was sitting near a stove in a deep trance.

At this time she claimed to be a sixty-three-year-old woman, Katrina Hogan. Later Katrina seemed to fade into Willie Cunning, a wayward youngster who had passed away.

Getting nowhere with Lurancy's constant changing of identity, Dr. Stevens suggested to her that the spirits that controlled her might send someone more rational and intelligent so that she might have more control over herself. Lurancy replied that there were many who would like to come, and she proceeded to name a list of people who had been dead for quite some time, and whom, in life, she (as Lurancy) had never known.

When Lurancy had finished recounting the eerie roster of souls, she said, "But there is one whom the angels have chosen . . . Mary Roff. She will come."

Roff was overcome with excitement. "Oh yes, let her come!" he said, thinking of his daughter who had died twelve years before.

When Lurancy awoke the next morning, she recognized none of the Vennums. She insisted that she was Mary Roff and begged her "father" (Roff) to take her home. Roff was dissuaded from such a move and Mary-Lurancy remained with the Vennums.

A short while later, Mary's mother and sister were on their way to the Vennum home to see Mary-Lurancy. Upon seeing the two relatives Lurancy embraced them and called her sister by the pet name "Nervie," which only Mary Roff had ever used.

This confrontation seemed to make the child even more homesick than before, so a move was agreed upon, and on February 11, 1878, "Mary" was allowed to go to the Roff home and stay.

During her sojourn in the Roff home, "Mary" recognized every person that she had known while she had been alive, from twelve to twenty-five years before. Lurancy-Mary also recalled many incidents which had occurred while she was still alive. The girl never seemed to recognize the Vennums until after they had made several trips to visit her and the two families had become close friends.

Then, in May of that same year, the girl told Mrs. Roff that Lurancy Vennum was coming back. "Mary" closed her eyes as if being led into a trancelike state; then the change took place.

When the Lurancy personality emerged, she looked around and asked where she was. Mrs. Roff told her, and the distressed girl asked to be taken to her home. The transformation had only lasted for a few minutes when Lurancy again left and the Mary personality returned.

One of the most interesting incidents in the dual life of Lurancy-Mary occurred one afternoon when she stated that her brother, Frank Roff, should be carefully watched, for that evening he would become gravely ill and might possibly die if proper attention were not available. Frank, at the time, appeared quite healthy.

Dr. Stevens checked with the family that night and then proceeded on to a patient's house in "Old Town." It was expected that that was where he would spend the night, but for some reason, he returned, unannounced, to the Roff neighborhood to stay at a Mrs. Marsh's.

At about two A.M. Frank went into convulsions.

"Go get Dr. Stevens," cried Lurancy-Mary. "He's at Mrs. Marsh's."

"No," the family argued, "he's in 'Old Town.'"

"He's at Mrs. Marsh's," the girl insisted, and, indeed, that is where the physician was found.

When Dr. Stevens arrived on the scene, he found Mary already treating her brother. She seemed to be doing everything quite properly, so he allowed her to continue under his guidance.

As time passed, the personalities occasionally attempted to alternate, the Mary dominance receding, permitting Lurancy to come through faintly. The changes were never complete enough to either totally obliterate the Mary personality or permit a full manifestation of the Lurancy personality.

Then one day Mary became quite disconsolate. "Lurancy is coming back," she said, and she gave a date and time.

The Mary personality immediately set about getting ready to leave, bidding farewell to friends and relatives. On the prescribed day, she and Mr. Roff were on their way to the Vennum house when the transformation took place. Upon arriving at her own home, Lurancy recognized all of the members of her family and seemed to show no ill effects from her experience.

On January 11, 1882, Lurancy married a farmer, George Binning. The Roffs visited her frequently, both before and after her marriage, and up until the time when she and her husband moved farther west in 1884.

In a letter to the *Religio-philosophical Journal,* Mr. Roff wrote that, for a time, "Mary" would take control of Lurancy for brief periods and then recede again. "Aside from this, she had little opportunity of using her mediumship, her parents being afraid to converse with her on the subject lest it should cause a return of the 'spells' . . . and her husband never made himself acquainted with spiritualism. . . .

"She has never had any occasion for a physician since she left us, never having been sick since then. . . . With the birth of her first child, Lurancy became entranced, and did not recover consciousness until after the child was born."

Later, physical researchers made attempts to get some statements directly from Mrs. Lurancy Binning, but no answer to the inquiries was ever received.

Perhaps in the case of Lurancy Vennum we might find a model case study of temporary possession and use it as a guide by which we might distinguish between cases of possession and cases suggestive of reincarnation.

To briefly summarize the case, we recall that Mary Roff had died when Lurancy was but fifteen months old. Although the two families lived in the same town, they were only slightly acquainted. During the period in which the Mary personality possessed Lurancy, she not only displayed the personal characteristics of Miss Roff, but she exhibited a knowledge of Mary's life which would have been quite beyond the capacity of either Lurancy or her parents. The Roffs themselves were convinced that their daughter had returned in the body of Miss Vennum. One knows how readily eager-to-believe parents might be momentarily deceived in the dim light of a séance room, but the Roffs were able to live with "Mary" for a period of several months. At no time did she falter in her knowledge of incidents and people with which she would have been acquainted as Mary Roff.

And at no time did "Mary" claim to be a past life of Lurancy Vennum. "Mary" had temporarily returned in Lurancy Vennum's body, and she spoke of Miss Vennum as a separate and distinctly different personality. (The same thing was true in the Dave Dean communications. At no time did the frontiersman claim to be a previous life of William Thatcher, the medium.)

This element of behavior on the part of the surviving or communicating personality seems to offer the investigator the principal difference between temporary possession and cases suggestive of reincarnation. At no time, in cases where the percipient of the experience seems truly to recall a prior life, does another personality claim to be utilizing the body of the percipient as means of communication. In true cases suggestive of reincarnation, the percipient claims to remember how he once felt and reacted to his environment in a previous life.

A case similar to that of Mary Roff–Lurancy Vennum, in which a separate personality controlled or possessed the body of the percipient, is that of Iris Farczady, a fifteen-year-old girl in Budapest, who seemed to have been "reborn" as a Spanish charwoman.

"Iris is dead," Mrs. Farczady told Cornelius Tabori, a well-known psychic investigator, when he arrived for an interview with the family in 1933. "She left us in August. She who lives with us now is called Lucia—a woman from Madrid."

Mr. Farczady was a chemical engineer. His wife was the daughter of a distinguished Viennese officer. Such a respected family as the Farczadys would seem to have nothing to gain and much to lose by attempting to perpetrate a hoax.

Mrs. Farczady told Tabori that she had always prided herself on being an enlightened, level-headed woman. Her daughter Iris had been a brilliant pupil—

an outstanding mathematician and linguist who had studied French and German.

"Then, that night in August, she felt ill. I put her to bed and sat with her. Suddenly she gave a long sigh. Somehow I knew that my darling, clever daughter had died.

"I bent over to listen to her heart; it was still beating. But I was right. My daughter had died. The person who had taken her body awoke, shouting in some foreign tongue. We tried to calm her, but she did not understand us. She jumped from the bed and tried to run from the house. She kept mentioning Pedro and Madrid. At last we realized that she was speaking Spanish."

Try as the family would to communicate with Iris, she would speak only Spanish. She could neither understand nor speak a single word of Hungarian, French, or German. It took the concentrated efforts of the large Farczady clan to teach her enough German so that they might be able to converse with her.

Tabori addressed Iris in German and received an angry protest because he had not called her by her "real" name.

"My name is Lucia Salvio," she corrected him in her heavily accented German. During the interview, she explained to the investigator that she had felt very ill that August afternoon in Madrid. Her husband, Pedro, had been away at work. When Lucia realized that she was dying, her first concern had been for her fourteen children—one for each year of her married life.

Mrs. Farczady commented to Tabori on the great diversity of temperament between her serious, studious Iris and the gay Lucia, who sang and danced for them.

"When I first looked into the mirror after coming here I was shocked," Lucia-Iris told the researcher. "I wondered what had happened to me and where my black eyes and thick dark hair had gone. Now I find it quite pleasing that in my new life, I am such a lovely young girl. My only regret is for my poor motherless children."

To seek substantiation for the bizarre story from a member outside of the immediate family circle, Tabori later visited Dr. Tibor Huempfner, a Cistercian professor who had spent many years in Madrid. The professor remarked that he had been astonished when the girl spoke Spanish to him and described the churches of Madrid in great detail. Huempfner had also been present at a party where Iris-Lucia had amazed a Spanish teacher by speaking to him in a perfect Madrid dialect.

The case of Concetto Buonsignore is also one of such complete possession by a controlling entity that the percipient lost his ability to speak in his native tongue. Buonsignore, a Sicilian peasant, awoke one morning speaking ancient Greek in the voice of one who had been dead for 2,700 years. Again, at no time, did the "voice" claim to be recalling a previous existence of the simple farmer.

Thinking that her husband had been overtaken by a spirit, or at the very least become insane, his wife motioned for him to follow her, and she led him to the priest of the small Sicilian town. The peasants, who greeted him along the way, were astounded to hear him babble back unintelligibly, as if he did not know them at all. After a moment's concern, they shrugged it off as the aftereffects of the previous evening's festival.

After listening to the man, the priest realized that he was not simply mouthing meaningless prattle. "Your husband is speaking in some strange language," he informed the wife of Buonsignore.

"What language?" the wife asked with a scowl. "He's never been off Sicily!"

But the priest was convinced that the old peasant farmer was speaking in some unfamiliar tongue. He sent for Father B., stationed in Palermo, who was a professor of literature and had great facility with languages. The priest came to Pergusa and listened carefully as Concetto Buonsignore spoke.

The linguist immediately announced that the man was speaking in Greek—though it was a variety of a very ancient dialect that the scholar had only come across in the Greek of Homer and his contemporaries.

After listening for a while longer, Father B. came to the astonishing conclusion that the Sicilian peasant was reliving a personality that was twenty-seven centuries old!

The first time that Concetto Buonsignore had even heard of Greece was when his son was sent to that country with an expeditionary force of the Italian army in World War II. But, as the Sicilian spoke to Father B., he described the surroundings and the times of the ancient city of Athens.

His house, he claimed, was in front of the altar and the temple of Demeter, and the dwelling was shaded by a large tree. He described a distinguished military career in which he had fought for his city-state as a soldier and a sailor. The priest was able to identify one of the battles in which he had taken part as the Battle of Aegospotami in 405 B.C.!

The "voice" went on to describe in correct detail how the Athenians had lost the naval battle by not heeding the words of Alcibiades, and how, the following year, Sparta had been able to dissolve the Athenian empire because of the loss of the fleet.

Concetto Buonsignore quickly became a celebrity, and newsmen began to converge on the island of Sicily and on the town of Pergusa.

The journal *La Domenica del Corriere* did print a long article reviewing the strange manifestation in its December 29, 1946, issue. The Milan reporter was one of the few who had arrived in time to hear the peasant use the ancient Greek tongue.

On the fifth day of possession, the personality of the ancient Greek sailor left the body of Buonsignore as suddenly as it had come. The last words spoken in the ancient tongue were directed at his wife: "I feel hungry." From that time on, the peasant lapsed back into his original personality and to the Sicilian dialect that he had spoken from birth.

The actual conversations that occurred between the Pergusa priest and the peasant farmer, while Buonsignore was in the entranced state, were recorded, witnessed, notarized, and filed with the French Academy of Sciences in Paris. The language professor, Father B., called in from Palermo, also signed the document as a witness.

And then there are those who voluntarily offer themselves as temporary physical dwellings for those who have "passed over." Especially in the phenomenon known as spirit healing do we find individuals who allow their bodies to be possessed by the alleged spirits of deceased physicians so that the great healers' work might be continued.

Dona Silvina, one of Portugal's most well-known witches, receives more than 100 clients a day. Her tiny house sometimes becomes so crowded that apprentice witches distribute numbered cards at the entrance, supermarket style, and Dona Silvina treats patients in groups of five.

Several pairs of crutches hang on the wall in silent testimony to the cripples who have been cured after a visit to the twentieth-century witch. Dozens of letters from grateful patients swell the files of this most unusual clinic.

The portly witch takes no credit for herself. "Everything that I give comes from my hands. They transmit the good wishes of the good doctor, Dr. Sousa Martins."

Dr. Sousa Martins died seventy years ago after a life of unselfish work among the poor people of Portugal. Dona Silvina claims that she allows the spirit of the doctor to "incarnate" within her and to use her body as an instrument by which he might continue his ministry of healing.

Dona Silvina invokes the incarnation of Dr. Sousa Martins by repeating a set speech: "Let us thank our brother, Dr. Sousa Martins, for the cures he is about to give us."

Once the invocation has been uttered, the witch goes into convulsions near her altar. The patients who have come to seek the curative gifts of the spirit doctor also begin to writhe about on rugs which have been scattered on the floor.

When the spirit has arrived to possess the witch, Dona Silvina sits on a low chair beside her creaky iron bed. From deep within her throat comes a manly growl which is allegedly Dr. Sousa Martins' voice.

"I miss the earth," the voice tells those assembled. "I miss my sick patients."

Once incarnated in the ample flesh of Dona Silvina, the spirt of the doctor wastes little time. At once, he sets about prescribing healing rituals and calling forth various patients to be cured.

For those patients who claim to have benefited from the bizarre clinic of Dona Silvina, it matters little that they have allegedly been treated by a doctor who has been dead for over seventy years.

CHAPTER FOURTEEN:
DREAM LOVERS AND SOULMATES

For centuries man's love ballads have included a good many melodies whose lyrics tell of dream lovers, who, the songs promise, will one day materialize as lovers of warm and acquiescent flesh. According to some men and women, their real-life experiences substantiate the promises made by those romantic songs and prove that a seed of love planted in a dream can someday produce a mature and lasting relationship. In this chapter we shall explore case histories of certain individuals who claim to have been haunted by a dream lover for years, until, one day, the very image of their nocturnal mate appeared before them as a very real human being.

Fred A. had his adolescent love life, which in nearly every teen-ager is fraught with emotional storms, further complicated by a vivid dream that he had when he was sixteen.

He had never been far off his parent's farm in Nebraska, but in his dream he was walking along a road that led to an old covered bridge that spanned a small creek. It was a beautiful autumn day, and multicolored leaves lay piled everywhere. As he crossed the bridge, he could see an old stone farmhouse, quite unlike anything that one would find in Nebraska. Boldly he entered the kitchen of the house, where he found a lovely

young girl with long blonde hair. She was dressed plain-
ly, but she was possessed of a natural beauty that did
not require the accentuation of elegant clothing. She
smiled at Fred, a warm, loving smile, than began to
walk toward him, her softly curving hips moving sen-
suously under the fabric of her cotton dress.

"Because it was a dream," Fred A. noted with amusement, "she walked right into my outstretched arms. It
seemed as though we had known each other for years.
We kissed; we hugged; we were delightfully happy in
each other's arms. I called her by name, and she whispered my name over and over again.

" 'Don't keep me waiting too long,' she said, becoming anxious when I said that I must go. 'I'll wait as long
as I can, but don't keep me waiting too long!' "

The dream left Fred feeling strangely warm and ex-
hilarated. There was a girl waiting for him somewhere.
What did pimples on his face and petty quarrels with
the girls in his class matter now? Somewhere his true
love waited for him.

But, at the same time, Fred felt terribly lonely.
Where was the girl now when he needed her? There
were proms and picnics and dances to attend right then.

"I knew that I had to put the dream girl out of my
mind," Fred recalled. "I dated a lot of really wonderful girls, but at the oddest and sometimes most inop-
portune moments, my thoughts flashed back to that
beautiful dream image. In my dream I had said her
name, but upon awaking I could remember it only as
something like 'Brenda'; but I knew that was not correct."

When World War II broke out, Fred enlisted and was
sent overseas to England. "My dream went with me,"
he stated in an account of his dream lover which he
prepared for interested researchers. "I certainly did not

lead a monklike existence, but while my buddies were forming steady relationships and some were taking war brides, I found myself haunted by my dream mate. How often did I argue with myself that I should marry some nice English girl rather than sit alone at night in the canteen, brooding over what may only have been the figment of some fantasy. Certain of my close friends began to wonder what was eating me, but I never dared to tell them. They probably would have had me out on a mental discharge."

Fred was discharged in 1945, and through a mix-up in his papers, found himself stranded in New York City for a few days. A buddy of his from Vermont invited him to spend the weekend at his folks' farm. After nearly four years in London, New York City held no big thrills for him, so Fred decided to accept his friend's offer. He had never seen a New England farm before, and a taste of rural living would help recondition him for Nebraska.

"It was my time for mix-ups, it seemed," Fred continued. "Jim's folks were supposed to pick us up at the bus depot, but when we arrived there was no one there. Jim had left the message with his seven-year-old brother, and he feared that the word might not have been relayed to his parents. 'It's only a couple of miles out of town,' Jim grinned. 'It's a beautiful day, and it might feel good to stretch our legs after that bus ride. Mind walking?' "

The two ex-soldiers had not hiked far when Fred had the strangest feeling that he had walked along that country road once before. Then they turned a corner, and he saw the old covered bridge that he had seen in that haunting adolescent dream. It was the same kind of startlingly lovely fall day, and the leaves were piled just as he remembered them.

"I knew that around the next bend we would see that old stone farmhouse, but what I had not guessed was that the place would be Jim's home. He led me through the back door into the kitchen. My heart was thudding so hard that I thought I would faint. I knew she would be there in the kitchen, and she was. An eighteen-year-old girl in a plain cotton housedress turned to smile at us from the sink where she was peeling potatoes. Her long blonde hair swirled about her face as she ran to give Jim a warm kiss of welcome. 'Hey, Fred,' Jim laughed, freeing himself from the girl's embrace, 'meet my kid sister, Brenna.'"

So it had been Brenna, not Brenda, Fred thought to himself. But he was too tongue-tied to say much of anything. The lovely blonde who stood before him, Jim's sister, was the girl of his dream.

"Brenna and I were in love before dinner that night," Fred concluded his account. "I will always remember her first words of love to me: 'Fred, darling, I've waited all my life for you.' Today we are as much in love as we were on our honeymoon, and we have four children as physical proof of our love. I shall never be able to explain that remarkable dream. At the time that I first saw my 'dream girl,' she was only about twelve years old; yet I saw her as vividly as if she had been in the flesh, and just as she appeared on the day that I actually, physically, walked into her life."

Martin J. saw his dream lover when he was in college, and he did not have long to wait before he met her in the wide-awake world.

"I knew my ribs cracked when the two fullbacks from ——— State creamed me," Martin said. "I blacked out, and I saw this pretty black-haired chick standing laughing at me. 'Clumsy,' she laughed. 'You should be more careful. I'm just going to have to look after you.' Then I opened my eyes and saw the coach bending over me. He wasn't nearly as pretty as the chick in my dream, but at least he wasn't laughing at me. A couple of the guys helped me off the field. The crowd yelled a noisy tribute to the fallen gladiator, but I knew that I was one Saturday hero who had been benched for a good while.

"The team doc taped my ribs, but he told me that he wanted me to go to the hospital on Sunday and get X rays, just to be sure. The next day I got this chick I had been going with to drive me out to the hospital. I left her sitting in the car, and I walked kind of cautious-like up the stairs. My ribs hurt.

"I was walking down the hallway to X ray when I saw this really groovy bird in her white nurse's outfit coming toward me. I knew there was something familiar about her, but before my brain could put it all together, I actually walked into a water cooler. The pain in my ribs was terrible, and I fell to the floor. When I looked up, this gorgeous nurse had her hands on her hips and was laughing at me. I almost mouthed the words along with her as it all came back to me. 'Where are you going?' she asked me. I told her, 'X ray, ma'am,' and she laughed again and said, 'Clumsy, you should be more careful. I guess I'll just have to walk along with you and look after you.'

"Later I talked an intern into running out to tell my girl that I had to be held for a while for observation. Ruth, the nurse, and I went out that night, and we plan to be married right after my graduation."

Irene Turnbull Mikolaizyk had been widowed for three years following the death of her husband, James

McCliggott, when she decided to leave Saginaw, Michigan, and go to live with her sister in Flint. Although her sister tried her best to make Irene feel welcome, the new widow continued to feel lonely and frustrated. She knew that life should not end for a healthy woman when she was only fifty-one.

One night shortly after her arrival in Flint, Irene had a vivid dream in which she was back in Saginaw, living in a small house. It was a Sunday in her dream, and she was on her way to church. As she passed a gasoline station, she realized that she needed some change for the collection plate. The manager of the station was a friendly, middle-aged man who was glad to accommodate her. They visited a few moments, and Irene learned that his name was Frank, that he, too, had lost his mate, and that he was a member of the church she was going to attend for the first time. He asked if he might accompany her some Sunday, and Irene expressed her consent to such a plan, adding that he should stop by for a cup of coffee sometime. In her dream, she saw Frank coming to her house, saw them keeping company for a time, then saw them being married in the church in the autumn.

Whether the dream had a contributing factor on Irene's decision to return to Saginaw remains unimportant to her today. On her third trip back, she found just the house for which she had been searching, and within a week she had moved into her new home.

"Come Sunday, I started walking to church," she wrote in the October 1964 issue of *Fate*. "I got the thought to check my money for the collection, and found that I had to have a bill changed. I went into a gasoline station, and the middleaged man that made my change seemed strangely familiar to me. His name was

Frank Mikolaizyk. Everything worked out exactly like it had in my dream. We were married in the fall when the leaves were coming down. . . ."

A psychic told me of a handsome client of his who had always been extremely popular with the opposite sex, but who had reached the age of thirty-three with his bachelor status intact.

"I used to tease him," the psychic said. "I used to ask him just what he was looking for. I would name each of the girls I had seen him with and enumerate all of their good points. Then I would challenge him to choose one of them for his wife. 'No,' he would tell me. 'Somehow I will know when I have found the right girl. She will be the girl that I once married in a dream.'

"At last, almost overnight it seemed, the rascal got himself married. He called me from a nearby city and told me that he had not needed my psychic impressions about this girl. He had met her while on a business trip and had fallen instantly in love with her. On the second day of their whirlwind courtship, he had said to her, 'I know you. We were married in a dream that I had when I was twenty.' The girl had replied: 'And I know you. I had that same dream when I was fifteen. You were the groom, and I have been searching for you ever since.' "

There will be some who will say that such dreams are the result of the Soul's yearning for its true soulmate, whose identity and whereabouts are known to the transcendent level of the unconscious mind. This information somehow manages to bubble up to the conscious mind during that altered state of consciousness which we call dreaming. The image of the soulmate thereby becomes an object of idealized love to the dreamer, and he becomes obsessed with searching for the lover whom he has glimpsed in the shadow world of his dreams. Others will inject elements from the reincarnation hypothesis into accounts of dream lovers come true and will maintain that certain mates must be sought out in order that patterns of Karma may be fruitfully played out.

The gifted Chicago psychic Teddy O'Hearn had the following to say about man's search for the divine soulmate:

"Mark this well, there is a great tapestry being woven as each of us entwines our lives with the other in our journey through the earth. This tapestry is, at one and the same time, a record of the past, as well as a means for each thread—each person—to evolve and to reach that perfection in an evolution which will free the individual from earth's tapestry, and the further necessity of returning to its travail. Woven into this tapestry are ugliness, horror, agony, suffering, and tears, as well as beauty, joy, a measure of fulfillment, and happiness. As in all of nature, nothing is ever lost.

". . . Only by experiencing the depths of what is inherent in the lowest can we reach the heights of the mystical ecstasy (union with God and our divinely ordained other half, our soulmate) which transcends beyond imagination anything possible in earthly experience.

"Regardless of the name one bears in any one earth lifetime, each of us has the eternal 'I' which carries either the male or female connotation of the androgynous being which we all were in the beginning, before Adam and Eve.

"The separation of the sexes came at that point in time depicted by the Bible's symbolic story of Adam, wherein God made the androgynous Adam two—male and female, negative and positive, Adam and Eve.

"At this time, earth's beings evolved into self-consciousness. This was not a fall from grace, but a further step in human evolution in order that the male and female counterparts of each entity might experience and learn and eventually be reunited when they had evolved through the testing of earth experience and attained the point at which each has earned the right to a reunion with his divine other half. This is the true soulmate, the only 'other' that each of us can look forward to meeting one day. It is with the soulmate that we will share complete fulfillment, a fulfillment beyond anything which we may ever know in any relationship on earth.

"Our conscious mind may have long since forgotten its soulmate, but the soul memory we have of our divine 'other half' filters through, though dimly, to our consciousness and leads us to a constant yearning and searching for complete and loving fulfillment which may continue life after life. It is this search which provides us with the means whereby we learn that love is not possession, that love is not self-serving, that love is not tyrannical or cruel, that love is not sex alone in any of its ramifications.

"We learn by trial and error through many loves and many lives, often encountering the same mates over and over again. All of these mates are soulmates by reason of the mutual learning process which takes place, but they must not be confused with the divine soulmate, both halves of which are seldom encountered in the physical earth plane. Each of these earthly soulmate relationships must be transmitted, from disharmony to harmony, into true universal love.

". . . We must learn real love through countless lifetimes of giving and receiving, of dealing with imitations and misconceptions of the real thing, of learning to cope with enmity, in order to achieve a complete education in lovemaking which will make us fit for the reunion with the divine soulmate.

"Thus in our searching and learning process we encounter many of the same 'loves' over and over again— sometimes as parents, as sisters, as brothers, as children, as friends, as enemies, as business associates, as teachers, as students, as well as lovers and husbands and wives. Our relationship with any one other individual is a learning experience and a perfection of the many facets of love. When we have learned and earned the right, we will begin to realize that love is indeed universal, rather than personal, that love, tempered by wisdom, is the tool we have to carry with us in our release from our earth lives. When we progress to the next step on the ladder and achieve the reunion and the fulfillment of self in the personal love of our divine soulmate, the two of us, as one, will go on into the fulfillment of ourselves in the work of the Father.

"So you see, we are all of us 'haunted lovers.' Our search for our divine soulmates makes us so."

Herewith is a teaching Francie, channel for Starbirth, received from her Parent-Guide relating to the role of soulmates in the coming time of transformation prevalent in the New Age dawning:

We all possess a Soul. Our Soul sends forth an energy into a living being to experience life on the Earth plane. This being is but a fragment of the Soul. This physical fragment is, on its own, without depth and incapable of *true* love. It is insensitive and is given to thoughtless actions. The fragment must learn to reflect its Soul. It must grow to develop sensitivity. It must come to express a genuine affection for all living things in order to permit more of its Soul to manifest in this life.

Very few fragments reflect their Soul; but for those who do, it is the ideal state of being, the result of much effort being expended by the fragment toward attaining the higher vibrations of love, knowledge, and wisdom. On the Earth plane, however, reflecting one's Soul can have its drawbacks, for it is extremely difficult to find like-minded fragments.

Those fragments who do reflect their Soul become appalled at the anger, hatred, disrespect, and ugly behavior of the physical fragments who live without reflecting their Soul. Therefore, those who reflect their Soul become lonely, bewildered, and unable to share the depth of their beautiful thoughts of loving ways with others. They feel unfulfilled and find no relationship that is total.

But there is a New Age dawning in which opposites will no longer attract; polarities will not be involved; friction will not be needed. This New Age will be one in which those who are alike will gather together. Evolved fragments will find their Soul-reflecting counterparts. The joy that will come from such unions will be without boundaries. Male and female counterparts will truly share and expand in all their thoughts, words, and actions, going forth together to accomplish a common goal that will benefit others. They will become whole and experience the heights of true ecstasy. They will understand the full meaning of that oft-spoken phrase, "And they shall become as one flesh." They will become a union of like-minded fragments which reflect their Soul. They will be the true Soulmates.

CHAPTER FIFTEEN:
OTHER LIVES, OTHER LOVES

There is, perhaps, no tale quite so romantic as that of reincarnation lovers who once again manage to find each other over the span of centuries. Unfortunately, it seems that the joy in encountering a remembered love is largely relegated to fictional romances. Among those individuals who claim real-life reunions with past loves from other lives, personal anguish, rather than personal happiness, appears to be the most commonly experienced emotion. Although some men and women have entered into happy marital unions as a result of a conviction that they had been sweethearts, lovers, or spouses in a past life, many reincarnated lovers feel that such an awareness of past intimacies with others has miserably complicated their lives with their present-life mates.

"I know that William and I must have a terrible Karma to work out," a buyer for a large department store wrote this author. "I am happily married and have been for ten years. Joseph is a very understanding husband, so understanding that he would listen to me explain to him about William."

The woman, whom we shall call Diana, had been haunted by a recurring dream ever since her early adolescence. In the dream she saw herself dying of a fever in a rudely built cabin. A man stood at the foot of her bed, looking down on her with distaste. He seemed afraid, as if she had some dread disease to which he in no way wanted to be exposed. He turned his back to her, walked out the door. Then Diana saw the flames crackling up around her bed.

"At this point I would awaken, screaming my terror and sorrow," she said. "I knew that the man was my husband. I knew that we lived in a crude cabin and that before he deserted me, he set fire to the cabin to destroy both me and my disease."

Diana led an active adolescence and was in no appreciable way inhibited by the dream, which she considered a memory of a past life. She had a morbid fear of fire and was perhaps overly concerned about communicable diseases—she would go to great lengths to avoid contact with anyone who suffered from so mild an affliction as a cold—but such idiosyncrasies would not unduly cripple one's social development. She married soon after her graduation from college, and her union with Joseph soon produced two daughters. Then she met William.

"He was getting off an elevator when I first saw him," Diana said. "His eyes seemed to pierce me to my very essence. I stood as if I had been turned to stone. Those were the eyes I had seen so often in my dream. A strange rush of both love and hatred filled my trembling body. I wanted to kiss him and strike him down at the same time. Somehow I managed to push past him and get into the elevator.

"When I returned to my office, I was shocked to find him waiting for me. I know that I must have paled, and I could not even find the intelligence to ask him his business. He seemed oblivious to my discomfort. He stood, flashed me a professional smile, and introduced himself as the new salesman for one of our largest suppliers.

"I mumbled something, sat down weakly behind my desk. I wanted to laugh at the way fate had strangely reversed our positions. If I chose, I could cancel our order with that company and virtually destroy the man's career.

"William had been studying me. 'I know this will probably sound like a standard salesman's line'—he grinned—'but don't I know you from somewhere?' "

That night over dinner Diana refreshed William's memory. When she confronted him with the memory of his desertion, he seemed contrite, anxious to make some kind of reparation for a misdeed long done. Diana is convinced that she has been reunited with William in order that he might work out his Karma and pay his debt for deserting her in another life. Diana has the memory of a recurring dream to fortify her conviction. I am not so certain that William remembers that past life, or if he is a clever opportunist who sees a way to make his present life a bit more interesting. And I am not at all convinced that Joseph can be taking this peculiar ménage à trois quite as matter-of-factly as Diana maintains. It is my impression that, rather than mending William's Karma, Diana is going to be breaking her marriage with Joseph.

A young assistant professor told me a much more convincing story of her rediscovery of a past love, as I waited to appear on a television talk show not long ago. She had gone to a stable to spend an afternoon horseback riding when she met a teen-age boy with whom she had an instant rapport.

"I looked at him and called him Wesley, and he

looked at me and called me Lillian. Neither of those names were our present ones, but they seemed to fit," she told me.

The two became good friends—only friends, she was quick to assure me, for "Wesley" was considerably younger than she. Each of them, however, felt strangely drawn to the other, and they became convinced that they had known each other in another life.

The psychic denouement came when "Lillian" dreamed that she was being threatened by an angry man. "It was too vivid to be only a dream," she maintained. "I can remember being dressed in a style that I associate with late frontier America. I got a name, a town in South Dakota, a state I have never visited in this life. I got a rush of apple orchards, a rural main street, parents, friends, and that furious man before me, my husband. He had found out about Wesley and me. In his rage, he threw an oil lamp at me. I screamed as the flames exploded onto my long skirt and crinolines. I was in terrible pain. Then I felt nothing, but I could see Wesley arriving too late to save me. I could see him trying to get to my room, but the flames had spread now, and he could not even climb the stairs. He stood there screaming my name.

"I watched him as he got his rifle from his saddle, sought out my husband, and shot him in the stomach. I was above everything watching, watching. I saw the funeral service that they held for my husband and for what little they could find that might be my remains. I also saw Wesley being hanged for the murder of my husband. My last emotion was feeling sorrow that my spirit could not join that of Wesley's when the rope jerked out his life."

At the same time that "Lillian" had been in the throes of her dream of remembrance, "Wesley" had to be awakened by his parents as he threshed about in the grip of a dreadful nightmare. Once they had managed to calm him, they told him that he had been screaming about a fire and how he must save Lillian.

"When we compared our dreams," the producer told me, "we found that we had both experienced a vivid recall of the life when we had been lovers. As we talked, we remembered other details, names, places, dates. I hope someday that I'll be able to travel to that town, which is now a city, and see how many things I can verify."

In an account submitted to *Fate* magazine's "My Proof of Survival" department for their August 1969 number, Arthur T. Huekendorff writes of an unusual occurrence which he witnessed when he was living in Shanghai in the 1920s as chairman of the board of the British-American Tobacco Company.

Yao Yu Tien, Huekendorff's close friend and business associate, had been left widowed and childless. Shortly after his wife's death, Yao told Huekendorff that a soothsayer had informed him that if he wanted many sons, he must marry a woman who was close to the earth. The seer gave Yao explicit instructions, and the businessman returned to Shanghai with a healthy eighteen-year-old bride who was already several months pregnant.

A few years later, after Yao's wife had presented him with two sons, the man confided to Huekendorff that his young wife had a most puzzling habit. On the average of one night a month, she would lie in bed and talk in a foreign tongue. Huekendorff's curiosity was aroused by his father's report, and he asked Yao to call him next time the incident occurred.

No more than a couple of weeks passed when Yao

called one night about 11:00. The young wife lay on the bed with her eyes open, but apparently unconscious of the presence of either Yao or Huekendorff. "She was silent," reads Huekendorff's account, "but after about fifteen minutes she burst into peals of laughter and then began to talk in French. My knowledge of French was not sufficient to enable me to understand what she was saying, especially as she was speaking very rapidly with all the mannerisms of a Frenchwoman, and in a voice quite unlike her own."

Huekendorff discussed the phenomenon with Dr. Fresson, his personal physician and a Frenchman. On the next occasion of the woman's weird "speaking in tongues," both Huekendorff and Dr. Fresson were in attendance.

This time the young woman's eyes were closed and she seemed unhappy. Tears streamed down her cheeks, and her speech was interrupted by violent bursts of sobbing. Dr. Fresson acknowledged that she was speaking in French, but he said that she was using many words that had passed out of contemporary usage. Her discourse had to do with the death and funeral service of a male friend or relative who was very dear to her. "My father will not survive this," she said repeatedly.

"She continued to talk for about half an hour, asking and replying to questions," Huekendorff concludes. When the young woman finally turned over on her side and fell into a deep sleep, Dr. Fresson found that her pulse was very slow. "A discarnate spirit returned, or moments from another life?" the narrator asks.

Huekendorff's question is one which every serious researcher asks himself as he makes a study of reincarnation. Are those stories which come from the lips of entranced subjects, regardless of how convincing they may be, really memories of past lives, or may a discarnate spirit be temporarily borrowing a voice box to tell his own story? Either phenomenon is remarkable, of course, but all that appears to be the recall of past lives may not really be reincarnation. Both phenomena do, however, seem to offer validation of the personality's ability to survive the death experience.

Recently a woman came up to me after one of my lectures and said that she suspected that her son was the reincarnation of a former lover, who had been killed in Korea. "Before he left me, he said that he would return. Even if he should be killed, he said he would come back to me," she told me. According to the woman, her son strongly resembled her deceased boyfriend, both in physical appearance and in disposition. The child was born three years after the man's death overseas.

I certainly have no easy answers to dispense to individuals who throw an enigma like that at me after a lecture. Could it really be a true instance of reincarnation? Or could the woman, dissatisfied with life as a mother and housewife, recall with great affection and yearning her deceased lover and in some unconscious manner be shaping her son to resemble the ghost lover of her memory more than his physical father?

Then there is the go-go dancer in the Indiana nightclub who swears that she is a reincarnation of an ancient temple love goddess. According to the pretty and shapely young woman, she was abused terribly by a high priest, who lowered her position to that of a temple prostitute. A group of drunken men seized her one night at her alcove in the temple and demanded that she surrender her body to them in accordance with her oath of love. They violated her body so roughly and so viciously that she developed an infection from internal injuries and died.

"I know that the high priest has also been reincarnated at this time," the attractive blonde says grimly. "I am seeking him out to kill him."

How will she know him?

"By his eyes. The eyes are the windows of the soul, and they never change."

And how will she kill him?

"The same way I was killed by those men when the high priest lowered my status in the temple. I will kill him with my body. I will love him to death!"

It is hard to say whether the young woman is actually convinced of her former life and her grim mission in the present, but in spite of medical assurances that one cannot die from too much lovemaking, the edge in her voice is enough to make all but the most foolhardy of men shelter his eyes when he speaks to her.

CHAPTER SIXTEEN:
THE MAN WHO RETURNED AS HIS GRANDSON

Mrs. Susan George was sorting through her jewelry box that afternoon when her son, William, wandered into her bedroom from the room in which he had been playing.

Fascinated by his mother's treasures, the five-year-old boy stood at the side of the bed where she had arranged her earrings, bracelets, necklaces, and pins. Then, spotting the gold watch which she lifted from the jewelry box, he suddenly reached out for the timepiece.

"William!" Mrs. George scolded. "Mustn't touch!"

"But it is mine!" the boy shouted. "That is my gold watch!"

"Shush," Mrs. George scowled. "That watch belonged to your grandfather. The same Grandpa William whose name you bear. He asked your momma to keep the watch for him."

"Yes," insisted William. "And that is my watch!"

The boy clung to the watch, and it took his mother several minutes to persuade him to allow her to replace it in the jewelry box. When Mrs. George told her husband, Reginald, about the incident, both of them were puzzled by the boy's behavior.

The Georges are Tlingit Indians who live in southeastern Alaska. Like other Tlingits, the Georges believe in reincarnation. Ever since their son William was born, he had given evidence of resembling his paternal grandfather in birthmarks, attitudes, and physical appearance. Although such things were within the realm of their personal beliefs, the Georges found that a manifestation of the doctrine of reincarnation occurring in their own home was more than a little disconcerting.

In his article, "Cultural Patterns in Cases Suggestive of Reincarnation Among the Tlingit Indians of Southeastern Alaska" (*Journal A.S.P.R.*, Vol. 60, July, 1966), Dr. Ian Stevenson analyzes the data of forty-three Tlingit cases. Surely the case of the fisherman who returned as his own grandson must rank as one of the most amazing and one of the most well-documented of contemporary studies of possible reincarnation.

William George I had been a well-known Alaskan fisherman, a healthy, robust man who had always been extremely active. As he grew older, the fisherman, in spite of the fact that he, like his fellow Tlingits, believed in reincarnation, began to experience certain doubts and uncertainties about the afterlife.

Often, when he and his favorite son, Reginald, were out fishing, the older man would say, "If there is really anything to this business of rebirth, I will come back and be your son."

On a number of occasions, William made such a statement to his daughter-in-law, Susan. Ignoring the laughter of the young people, the fisherman would expand his statement by saying that they would be able to recognize him by the fact that he would be reborn with the same birthmarks as the ones he presently bore. These birthmarks were well known by his friends and kin to be two large moles, each about half an inch in diameter, one on his upper left shoulder and the other on his left forearm.

William George continued to discuss his plans for a return to life in the form of Reginald's son, and he became increasingly serious about the matter. In the summer of 1949, he gave Reginald his gold watch.

"This was given to me by your mother, as you well know," William told his son. "I want you to take it now, and I want you to keep it for me. When I come back as your son, I'll reclaim the watch, so you take good care of it for me."

Reginald told his father not to dwell on such a morbid subject. The elder George was in fine health, sixty years old, and should be able to look forward to several more productive years. Reginald told his father to keep his watch and to plan to carry it for many years to come.

William George was insistent. "I don't have long, and I don't want any harm to come to the watch. If there is anything to this business of reincarnation, I'll be back as your son and I'll get my watch back then."

Reginald could see that there was no use in arguing further with his determined father. He went home for the weekend, told his wife what his father had said.

"You might as well go along with him," Susan George advised her husband. "I'll put his watch in my jewelry box. It'll be safe there."

A few weeks later, in August, the crew of William George's seine boat reported their captain as missing. None of them could say what had happened to their skipper. His body was never recovered, and they could only conclude that he had fallen overboard and had been swept away by the tide.

On May 5, 1950, scarcely nine months after William

George's death, his daughter-in-law, Susan George, went into labor.

As she lay in the delivery room waiting for the anesthetic that would remove her consciousness, Susan George thought she saw the form of her father-in-law standing at her side. The vision was so real and the action of the image so lifelike that Mrs. George came out of the anesthetic uttering soft cries of confusion. She awoke fully expecting to see an apparition of William George still hovering in her room.

Mrs. George saw no apparition, but she was presented with a healthy baby, a boy who had a large mole on his left shoulder and another on his left forearm. Both birthmarks were in precisely the same location as those borne by his grandfather.

Reginald and Susan George were confused. It seemed as though William George had returned just as he had promised. At any rate, the couple felt that the exact placement of the moles justified their naming their son William George II.

As the boy began to grow up, his parents found an ever-increasing number of details which tended to justify their decision to name their son after his grandfather. The boy's behavior traits, his likes, dislikes, and skills coincided exactly with those of William George I.

Foremost among the many similarities was the peculiar manner in which the boy walked. His grandfather, when a young man, had injured his right ankle severely while playing basketball. William George I had walked with a limp for as long as most members of the fishing village could remember. Because of the nature of the injury, William had turned his right foot outward so that he walked with a peculiar gait which became a characteristic of the man. Reginald and Susan George were startled when their young son took his first steps with his right foot turned outward. In spite of their efforts to guide the boy into a proper gait, he persisted in maintaining the peculiar, twisted manner of walking.

"He is the image of his grandfather," members of the George family have told investigators. "Not only does he look like him, he worries like him."

The Alaskan fisherman, for all his bravado and skill aboard his boat, was known as a great worrier. His constantly repeated words of cautionary advice to his crew often brought groans of irritation from seamen who felt that they knew their business at least as well as their captain. William I also had the habit of giving unsolicited advice to much older and more experienced seamen. When Dr. Stevenson investigated the case in 1961, the boy had gained the reputation of being fretful and overly cautious. It was especially noted that William II had a morbid fear of the water.

"But he certainly knows his fishing and his boats," one fisherman testified. "The first time he was put in a boat he already knew how to work the nets."

"And he knew all the best bays for fishing and how best to work them," another fisherman put in.

William George II has always referred to his greataunt as his sister. His uncles and aunts (Reginald's brothers and sisters) have always been his "sons" and "daughters." In gruff tones, he has scolded two of his "sons" (uncles) about their excessive use of alcohol. William's own brothers and sisters often call him "grandpa," a title to which he has never objected.

In recent years, William II has been discouraged from talking about his former life. Older members of the Tlingit village have warned his parents about the dangers of recalling a past life, and Reginald and Susan have heeded this advice.

"His mind had begun to wander," Reginald said. "He was becoming more concerned about the past than about the present and the future. This can be very harmful."

Although he has ceased to speak in excessive measures about his past life as his grandfather, William II still persists in asking for "his" gold watch.

"I should have it now that I am older," he maintains.

CHAPTER SEVENTEEN:
CAN WE REMEMBER OUR ANCESTORS' LIVES?

Can memory be inherited by genetic transmission?

The birth of a redhead in a family of brunettes is always the subject for a great deal of rather earthy speculation, until it is discovered that great-great-grandfather proudly wore a fiery mane and beard.

The unexpected appearance of musical talent in a family of folks "who can't carry a tune in a bucket" or a drunkard in a family of teetotalers may be due to memory-energy patterns transmitted in the genes.

If the miracle of conception, with its pairing of the mother-genes and the father-genes, determines the color of our hair and our eyes, our basic height and weight, our inherent strengths and weaknesses, is it not possible, many researchers are asking, that certain dramatic memory patterns may also be inherited?

In another of my books, I relate the story of how a young Jew in Ireland was "cured" of a crippled hand by the teamwork of a psychiatrist and a psychic sensitive. The sensitive determined that the young man's subconscious carried the violent memories of a pogrom in Czarist Russia. This particular persecution had included the rape of the young man's female ancestor and the chopping off of the hand of a male ancestor who had struck back at his attackers.

When the young man was told of the sensitive's impressions of the origin of his physical debility, he remarked to the doctor that it was as if he had heard it all before, long ago. Once the seat of the trauma had been discovered, its therapy could be prescribed along the lines of conventional psychoanalysis.

In his article "A Genetic Theory of Reincarnation," which appeared in *Fate,* Volney G. Mathison wrote that the precise knowledge of "how" we inherit physical and psychical characteristics remains a mystery to science. Some of the genes which we have by chance inherited may have least appeared in a remote ancestor. Incredible as it may seem, only twenty generations back, we each have 1,048,576 ancestors. Only forty generations back crowds the family tree with over 140 trillion ancestors. On cellular and bioelectronic levels, elements of all of these ancestors are within us, and vast amounts of data are carried in the minute storage area of the electrons.

Mathison theorizes that since our electronic patterns transmit detailed information about our forebears' physical structures, these patterns may also carry memory data relating, he says, to enforced genetic modifications of structure occurring as a consequence of lack of food, injuries in combat, pestilences, and other disasters.

Mathison believes that certain repetitive dreams or hypnotically induced recollection of past lives may be the reactivated expressions of harmful events suffered by some remote ancestor whose genes were inherited.

Obviously, not everyone walks around bent under with the sorrows of the trials and tribulations of his ancestors. What Mathison is postulating is that some individuals may experience disturbing present-moment situations which contain elements similar to the disastrous ancient events in their genetic line.

These, he suggests, trigger images, either symbolic

or actual, of those ancient, unknown past events which had decisive effects upon one or more of our forebears and, hence, inevitably upon us.

Perhaps such a theory of genetic memory explains the case of a man whom an analyst would refer to only as Harold.

Harold was of Scandinavian stock, and he worked a farm in the heart of rich Midwestern cropland. Since early childhood, Harold had had a morbid fear of fire. This phobia had reached such dramatic proportions that the child would run screaming from the room if a guest lit a cigarette.

Harold's crisis situation was reached when, as a young man of thirty-two, the barn on the family farm caught fire.

Harold's sixty-five-year-old father went into the flaming building in an attempt to lead a prize bull to safety. Timbers collapsed and both Harold's father and the animal were trapped in the flames.

As much as Harold wanted to go to his father's rescue, the young farmer was unable to move from the spot where he lay sobbing and vomiting upon the ground. Fortunately, neighbors arrived in time to rescue Harold's father. The bull had to be destroyed.

The analyst was perplexed because he could find no precipitating trauma in Harold's childhood which would account for his pyrophobia. According to his parents, Harold had "just been born afraid of fire."

This case does not end with a session of hypnotic regression probing the source of Harold's phobia. This particular analyst is much too conservative to employ such "farfetched" (and time-saving) techniques.

No, in this case it was the patient who provided the key to his problem. Or maybe that is what happens in any successful psychotherapy. At any rate, during one session, Harold brought with him an old leather-bound diary.

"It belonged to my great-grandmother on my mother's side," Harold told the analyst. "It is her journal of the trip across the ocean and her early days on the prairie."

Harold's family maintained close ties with relatives in the "old country," and Harold's parents were able to read Norwegian. The night before, the young man explained, his mother had had an unusual idea and had read aloud a certain section of the journal.

"My great-grandmother writes of a terrible thing that happened to my great-grandfather on the ship coming over," Harold said. "A fire broke out in the ship's galley, and a can of cooking grease exploded.

"Great-grandfather was seated near the galley door at the time, and some of the flaming grease landed on his chest, shoulders, and neck. He received very bad burns, and he nearly died before they reached America. Mother says that he bore the scars from those burns until the day he passed away."

The analyst slowly tapped the point of a pen on his note pad. "And you think there may be some connection between your great-grandfather's severe burns and your fear of fire?"

"Well," Harold said, "you know, it's a funny thing, but ever since I was a kid, whenever I would think of fire, I would get a picture of the sea. I could never make any association before. You know, fire and water, complete opposites.

"Then, last night, when Mom was reading from that old diary, I had this funny feeling. I could see it all as she read it, just like I was watching it all on television."

Had the memory, and thereby the fear, of fire been

transmitted through the genes from Harold's great-grandfather to his own memory bank?

Volney G. Mathison relates a strangely similar case of a fear of fire that had seemingly been transferred to a descendant by genetic memory.

Connie, a Mexican girl who was employed in Mathison's electronic plant, had been doing a clumsy job of soldering joints and wires. Apparently unaware of her shoddy workmanship, she became extremely upset and irrational whenever she was reprimanded by her supervisor.

Mathison knew that previous analysis had indicated that Connie had "an intense, subconscious terror of getting burned." According to conventional psychoanalytic theory, this meant that Connie had suffered severe burns in childhood or infancy. But she never had, as far as anyone could determine.

Mathison decided, rather reluctantly, to hypnotize Connie and try for a Bridey Murphy type of past-life regression.

While under hypnosis, the girl told of being en route to the New World on a Spanish sailing vessel! A fire broke out on the crowded seventeenth-century ship, and in the resulting panic, she had been badly burned.

When Mathison brought the girl back to the present, she exclaimed, "Why should I be so afraid of a little old soldering iron after I went through all that?"

It is interesting to note that the girl had a reddish birthmark that covered her back and her right shoulder. According to Mathison, this mark began to diminish in size after the catharsis of the hypnotic session.

A case which seems to be an instance of genetic memory becoming an obsession came to my attention a few years ago. It would seem to fit into our discussion in this chapter, although I will readily concede that the case might also be representative of possession, or, perhaps, an instance of extreme ancestor identification.

When Karl Woodstock married Joan, he decided that the perfect place to spend their honeymoon would be his grandfather's old hunting lodge in Northern Michigan. Karl's parents tried to dissuade him from using the old place. No one had used it in years, they argued, and it had fallen into a state of disrepair.

Karl's father had never cared for hunting or fishing and had not been to the cabin since his own father's death, when Karl was ten years old.

"I got enough of hunting and fishing and getting up at dawn every morning when I was a kid," he would say whenever Karl would beg to go north to the cabin. "I just got sick of it. Besides, spending a day with a fishing pole is like throwing a day away. You can never regain time wasted, boy."

Karl's grandfather had been a professional portrait painter of some repute, and the hunting lodge had been both his retreat and his favorite studio.

"Where better to work than amongst Nature?" Karl could remember his grandfather saying. "If my clients can't wait for me to get back to the city, they can come out here to have their portraits painted."

With Grandpa Woodstock, a vacation at the lodge was strictly a busman's holiday. He would rise at dawn for several hours of hunting or fishing, then he would spend the rest of the day at his easel, just as if he were in his studio in the city. The lodge walls were hung with portraits of the Indians, fishermen, hunters, trappers, and dairy farmers who were local residents of the area. These portraits were never for sale, although, on occasion, Karl had known Grandpa Woodstock to give one away to the subject who had patiently sat for him.

Karl's bride, Joan, was a game girl, who did an excellent job of convincing her husband that she would like nothing better than to spend her honeymoon reconditioning a hunting lodge in the north woods. Before their two weeks had ended, however, Joan Woodstock had come to regret the fact that she had not held out for the more conventional Bermuda or Niagara Falls.

On the first night in which they occupied the cabin, Karl found an old family album. The newlyweds were amusing themselves with the snapshots of the child Karl, when the young husband noted a photo of his grandfather with a luxuriant Van Dyke.

"I never knew Grandpa to wear a beard," Karl said. Then, reading the scrawled caption beneath the snapshot, he exclaimed, "No wonder. This was taken thirty years before I was born."

Karl rubbed his chin reflectively, then turned his attention to a number of notebooks which his grandfather had kept during his years of study in Paris. When Joan fell asleep that night, Karl was still reading the journals by the light of a blazing fire.

The new bride woke up alone that morning, a condition to which she would soon become accustomed. She found Karl at the end of the dock. He had risen early to go fishing.

That afternoon, Joan rubbed her cheek after a kiss, and asked Karl if he weren't going to shave. Karl grinned, replied that he had always wanted to grow a beard. Joan rolled eyes heavenward. A honeymoon seemed like a most unlikely time to begin to grow a beard.

When they went into the nearest town for some food supplies that evening, Karl disappeared from Joan's side for a few moments and returned bearing a sack of artist's supplies.

"I was glad that hobby shop had some oils and brushes," Karl said. "The tubes in the cabin have dried out."

"I didn't know you painted," Joan said. "Have you any other hidden talents?"

At the end of the two-week period respectfully set aside as the newlyweds' honeymoon, Karl's parents decided to drive up to the cabin and pay the young couple a surprise visit. The surprise, as it turned out, was on them.

Karl's father was shocked to see his bearded and besmocked son standing before an easel, while the long-suffering Joan sat in a swimming suit, posing for him. Scattered around the studio were a number of portraits in varying stages of completion.

The style in which the paintings were done, according to Karl's father, was that of his own father's early period. Karl's mother later testified to the fact that her son had not previously shown any desire to paint nor had he displayed any creative inclinations. Regarding Karl's physical appearance as he stood behind the easel with his rapidly sprouting Van Dyke, both parents remarked that they felt as if they were seeing a ghost of the boy's grandfather when they first entered the studio.

"Karl looks as Father did when he was young," the senior Woodstock stated. "He resembles Father as he was long before Karl was born."

Karl continued to paint after the young couple had set up housekeeping in their own apartment back in the city. As time passed, however, his painting became progressively worse, and Karl soon lost interest in the easel. Shortly thereafter he had abandoned his oils and brushes, and awoke one morning aghast at what he saw in the bathroom mirror. He immediately set about shaving off his beard.

This case, admittedly, contains a variety of factors which may have brought about Karl's temporary obsession. On the most simple level, we might conclude that Karl suddenly became interested in emulating his grandfather after spending a night reading his journals. This would not, however, account for the considerable talent which the young man originally displayed. A desire to imitate will not substitute for talent no matter how fierce the wish.

Reincarnation per se seems out of the question in Karl's case. Karl was a boy of ten when his grandfather passed away. Such a thing as temporary possession by the spirit of his grandfather could remain as a possible hypothesis.

On yet another hand, might not our theory of genetic transmission of memory be considered a very likely explanation? A memory of style, skill, and even appearance could have been transmitted through the genes—a memory that became intensified and stimulated by the young man's moving into an environment in which those memories would have been developed by the original percipients, Karl's father and grandfather.

Because sex is one of man's most basic and powerful drives and because sex is Nature's way of insuring mankind's physical immortality, Volney Mathison has discovered a number of cases in which a violent sexual experience has left a memory pattern that results in problems for future generations.

Mathison relates the case of a married woman whose every contact with her husband would produce in her a severe genital inflammation. This condition was extremely painful and would persist for days after sexual intercourse.

While in deep hypnotic trance, the woman told of a past life in which she had been raped repeatedly by a band of seacoast marauders. The terrible experience left her ancestor with painful injuries.

Mathison states that on the basis of this genetic dream, he "proceeded precisely as in the case of any severe present-life trauma or injurious situation."

In another of the hypnotist's cases, a woefully unattractive spinster was sent to him because she suffered from depression.

While under hypnosis, Mathison says, the woman told of being a beautiful, immoral, and ruthless courtesan who had ruined homes, driven men to duels, and inspired murders.

"I'm sixty-five and I'm still a virgin," the woman wailed to the hypnotist when they spoke of her present life. "No man has ever wanted to marry me, or wanted me at all . . . no man ever will. I'm the world's ugliest woman. This is my Karma. I'm paying for what I did in previous lifetimes."

Although Dr. Ian Stevenson admits that we have not discovered the limits of genetic transmission, he argues in his essay, "The Evidence for Survival from Claimed Memories of Former Incarnations," that the extension of such a hypothesis to account for the apparent memories of former incarnations meets with serious obstacles.

Dr. Stevenson concedes that genetic memory might apply in instances where the percipient (Person A) belongs to a line descending from Person B, but he points out that in most cases suggestive of reincarnation, the second person was born in another family and in another town. Dr. Stevenson also states that the second birth usually occurred within a few years of the death of the first person. This would make impossible any transmission of information from the first to the second person along genetic lines.

In this view, then, genetic memory may indeed be a possibility, but it has nothing to do with reincarnation. Unless, of course, one were to argue for a Jungian "collective unconscious," in which lie all memories, attitudes, and inclinations that have been amassed by the past of the human race, a collective unconscious into which the transcendent level of every human mind may dip and draw from according to individual need, desire, or longing.

CHAPTER EIGHTEEN:
THE MYSTERY OF NAOMI HENRY

In March 1956, Henry Blythe, a professional hypnotist, was commissioned by the *London Daily Express* to undertake a duplication of Morey Bernstein's experiments with "Bridey Murphy."

As his subject in the experiment, Blythe chose Mrs. Naomi Henry, a thirty-two-year-old housewife from Exeter. Mrs. Henry, the mother of four children, had proved to be an exceptionally good subject in past demonstrations. She went under hypnosis rapidly, entered an unusually deep trance state, and was very sensitive to Blythe's suggestions and commands.

In an early series of experiments with Mrs. Henry, Blythe felt that he had been able to project her astral self from her body and accomplish remarkable feats of telepathy.

In his book, *The Three Lives of Naomi Henry,* Blythe wrote that he had succeeded in taking Naomi's "self," "soul" or "spirit" out of her physical body. If he could reproduce this phenomenon before an audience, he would be in a position to prove that the "self" can leave the body and that therefore physical death need not be the end of everything because it was possible for the "self" to exist outside the human envelope which encased it.

According to Blythe, he and Naomi succeeded wonderfully well in their demonstrations before large audiences at St. Mary's Bay holiday camp, Brixham. Blythe did, however, note that Naomi seemed exhausted after each performance and called for several glasses of water. The hypnotist became concerned for the woman's health, as did her husband, and Blythe ceased to use Mrs. Henry as a subject in 1951.

But now, five years later, there was a new challenge. The *Daily Express* had offered £250 for evidence of an authentic case of reincarnation in Britain. Blythe had accomplished age regression with several subjects, and he felt that if anyone could recall a former life under hypnosis, as in the Bridey Murphy case, it would be Mrs. Naomi Henry.

On the afternoon of March 28, 1956, in the presence of four reporters, Blythe regressed Mrs. Henry as far back as her memory would go. The subject was commanded to tell those assembled whom she was and what she was.

After a pause, her voice softly acknowledged that she was "Mary."

During that first session, Naomi-Mary told the hypnotist and the representatives of the press that she was a seventeen-year-old Irish farmgirl from Cork named Mary Cohen (because of this unusual surname for an Irish family, the name was thought, perhaps, to be Coen, Cowen, or Cowan—names which would sound the same as Cohen when spoken). Naomi-Mary recalled that the farm on which she lived was called Greengates, that the nearest village was Grener, and that her greatest affection was directed toward her fifteen-year-old brother Sean.

The newspapermen were greatly impressed with

Blythe's initial success and greatly urged him to attempt to discover more details of the Mary-life during the next session.

It was because of their insistence that Blythe try to learn the details of Mary's death that a most terrible and frightening thing occurred during that next experiment.

Blythe had begun by taking Naomi-Mary back to her life at age twenty-seven. By this time, "Mary" had been married to a man named Gaul, whom she did not love, and had had two sons. When Blythe progressed the personality to age fifty, the hypnotist and the assembled witnesses noted the physiological change which seemed to come over Mrs. Henry. A pained expression distorted her features; her mouth pulled down at the corners, and she looked older. Her attitude was one of bitterness toward a brutal husband who beat her and mistreated their sons.

Blythe moved Naomi-Mary up to age sixty. At this stage, her speech became that of an old and senile woman. She was uncertain of her surroundings, vague about how old she was, and who was with her. She told Blythe that she was only able to hobble about on "sticks."

The hypnotist jumped ahead another ten years. The personality asked to lie down. Blythe assured her that she was lying down and need not fear.

He asked her how much longer she had to live.

Hoarsely the voice whispered that a woman said not long.

Then, after Blythe promised Naomi-Mary that things would soon be peaceful for her, the personality uttered, "Praise God!"

He was watching her closely, his fingers on the pulse on her left wrist, Blythe wrote of the session. Suddenly he felt her pulse die away, her breathing—clearly audible in the room during both sessions—stopped, every trace of color gone from her face. She appeared to be dead. He bent close to try and discover a trace of a breath, but there was nothing.

By urgently assuring Naomi-Mary that she was safe, Blythe managed to bring her out of the state of suspended animation into which she had entered.

Although Mrs. Henry bore no ill effects from her five seconds of "death," the *Daily Express* chose to remove their support from the experiments at once. On April 28, Donald Gomery wrote of his paper's decision to abandon the investigation.

Gomery related that a number of experiments across the whole of Britain, all conducted by professional hypnotists, had produced some startling results. Then he mentioned the chilling episode which had taken place during Blythe's second session.

That woman, he pointed out, had "died" at sixty-six. When the hypnotist asked what she was doing at seventy she realized that she was "dead." Then she stopped breathing.

That is why he felt the experiments should not continue—because he now believed that there lay danger.

He confessed that when the report reached him, he felt more than frightened: he felt acutely afraid although the experiment was carried out by a professional hypnotist of known ability in front of witnesses. He was afraid that publication of such experiments might induce others, not sufficiently qualified, to carry out similar experiments without proper supervision, experiments that might have a damaging effect on the subject.

Blythe could not argue with the *Daily Express* decision. He felt that it was a blow to discontinue the investigation, but he could sympathize with the newspaper's position if even one amateur hypnotist were to regress even one person and possibly his heartbeats as a result of having read the series in the *Daily Express*.

To Blythe's great joy, however, Mrs. Henry agreed to continue the experiments privately.

On May 18, in the hypnotist's consulting room, the investigation began its second session. Attending as witnesses were Mrs. Blythe; Dr. William C. Minifie, Osteopath; Douglas Warner, author; and Elizabeth Warner, who was given the task of shorthand reporter. Although a tape recording was made of nearly all the sessions, Mrs. Warner's notes were useful both as a check against the tapes and as an ever-alert human record. The tape recorder needed to have its spools changed and might be "deaf" at a crucial moment.

Blythe brought Naomi back to her life as Mary Cohen and the investigators learned additional facts about the Irish girl's existence.

Her parents had literally given the bride away in marriage to Arthur Gaul. Mary protested that she did not love her husband, but that her mother had told her she couldn't keep her any longer.

The only pleasantness which Mary could remember in her entire lifetime was the afternoons which she spent in the meadows with her younger brother Sean.

Her death had come on the floor of an old house. Two or three old women and one old man had witnessed her death. Mary's last days were spent in pain, hobbling about on sticks, because her husband beat her so severely that he had broken a leg.

When Blythe asked her if she were glad to have finished that life, she answered, "Oh, yes!"

Then the hypnotist posed a question which each of the investigators had been eagerly awaiting: What happened to her in between that life when she was Mary

Cohen and when she came back again to us . . . what was she doing in between that life and this?

Each member of the group leaned forward expectantly. Would they now hear details of what life was like after death? Would they at last be able to tell their fellow man what kind of existence he might expect beyond the grave?

"Nursing," came the answer.

The investigators shot one another bewildered glances. Blythe temporarily found himself at a loss for words. Her reply had been so totally unexpected that the hypnotist was forced to take a few moments to regain his control.

When he was once again able to direct his questions to the entranced subject, Blythe was startled to learn that he had uncovered yet another life of Naomi Henry.

In this life, the personality had been much happier. Her name had been Clarice Hellier, and she had been a nurse, who, at the turn of the century, had been responsible for the care of twenty-four children.

Clarice's life had been short and uneventful. She had died at thirty-two of a goiter in her throat, completely contented that her life had been spent caring for her wonderful children.

A crippled boy named Bobby had received the most attention from the nurse, and both Blythe and the other investigators noted the similarity between her love for Sean (in Mary's life) and her affection for the crippled Bobby. The comparison was brought into even sharper focus when the hypnotist regressed the personality back to Mary's life and they learned that Sean, too, had been a cripple!

During the fifth and last experiment, Naomi-Clarice was brought up to her time of death. She said she was at Westbury on Tyrm.

Blythe asked Clarice what she was doing at Westbury on Tyrm.

Clarice spoke slowly, squinting as if she were trying to read something which she could see but dimly. She hesitantly mentioned numbers, ending with the number 207!

Blythe asked her what the number meant.

There was a long pause, and the investigators leaned forward to catch the faint, single word "grave."

Clarice had been reading the number of her gravestone!

Then the voice was still. Blythe knew that this was the end of memory.

Gently the hypnotist spoke to Mrs. Henry and told her that the experiments were over. He assured her that he could take away every memory trace of what she had told them. She would go back to being her normal self. All memories of her previous existences would be wiped away, cleared from her mind and Soul. She would come back to them as a normal, ordinary woman.

In the conclusion to his book, Blythe lists seven hypotheses which might explain the three lives of Naomi Henry:

1.) that he perpetrated an elaborate hoax to gain publicity for himself;

2.) that Naomi Henry managed an ingenious deception;

3.) that the subconscious mind of the hypnotist placed the deception into the subconscious of Mrs. Henry;

4.) that the hypnotist dredged up a compilation of strange memories from the subconscious of Mrs. Henry;

5.) that malignant spirits brought about the hoax;

6.) that the revelation of past lives is a gift from the

spirit world to be used for mankind's enlightenment;

7.) that the experiments have proved reincarnation
—that is, the rebirth after death of one spirit
in the body of a new creation.

Blythe hopes that his reputation will serve to eliminate hypothesis number one from consideration. The
hypnotist believes that Mrs. Henry must certainly be
absolved. Not only does he consider the woman mentally and morally incapable of practicing a deliberate deception of such creative magnitude and histrionic ability,
but he points out that even the greatest actress could not
have stopped her pulse and breathing for five seconds
and frightened a great newspaper into calling off so
promising a series of investigations.

Blythe does give the third hypothesis its due, and he
admits that Douglas Warner, the author who served as
one of the witnesses, is inclined toward that particular
explanation. The hypnotist personally rejects this
theory, however, because he, in his experience, has
"never known the subconscious to act so 'out of character.' " For the same reason, Blythe discards the fourth
hypothesis.

As for the supernatural explanation postulated in the
fifth and sixth theories, Blythe admits that he has no
evidence to support spirit activity, but he concedes that
such phenomena "may be possible."

The seventh hypothesis, that reincarnation is fact,
Blythe feels may be supported by several confirming
items which were subsequently uncovered by private investigators assigned to gather evidence of the physical
existence of Mary Cohen and Clarice Hellier.

The hypnotist is most impressed by the fact that
Mary-Clarice-Naomi is recognizable through two centuries as basically the same person. If Naomi Henry

had revealed an existence in 1790 as the daughter of a king, the whole story would have been less credible, while as Mary Cohen and Clarice Hellier there is an essential rightness which puts no strain on credulity.

It must have been this essential "rightness" which prompted Annie Besant to write (in *The Ancient Wisdom*) that with reincarnation man is a dignified, immortal being evolving towards a divinely glorious end; without it, he is a tossing straw on the stream of chance circumstances, irresponsible for his character, for his actions, for his destiny.

Do the three lives of Naomi Henry prove reincarnation, with its evolution toward a "divinely glorious end"? Whatever hypothesis one wishes to accept at this point, the evidence amassed by Henry Blythe during the five sessions of hypnotically controlled regression must certainly be judged as most impressive. Whether the evidence offers substantial proof of reincarnation or another startling facet of mind, Blythe has made a great contribution toward the "final judgment."

CHAPTER NINETEEN:
THE METASOURCE RESEARCH ON PAST LIVES

"Metasource is interested in verifying—and that includes proving or disproving—a wide range of phenomena which are now called paranormal, mystical, or supernatural. If the institute has a bias, it is that there can be no bias.

"We found that some areas of the paranormal seem to have more validity or 'provability' than others. And some of these areas also seem to be more important in terms of their value to mankind, at least in their potential to help each individual live in a more productive way. We knew that an awareness and an acceptance of reincarnation could have a profound effect on an individual. We noted that people who underwent age-regression hypnosis and reexperienced past lives often began to adopt a new perspective. We saw people change their ideas of guilt and prejudice. We saw them begin to cope differently in their daily lives."

The speaker was an attractive, compactly built man in his mid-thirties named Shad Helmstetter, who is the director of Metasource Research Institute (P.O. Box 4817, Scottsdale, AZ 85258). Shad paused to light a long, slender, dark cigarette. That mundane act completed, he brushed the fingers of his free hand reflectively over his dark, well-trimmed goatee and continued speaking:

"Metasource was organized to explore, research, collect, and disseminate data of a metaphysical nature. We felt that the New Age person at some time in the future would very possibly use abilities such as telepathy or clairvoyance at will. These could be very useful tools. And there is a vast and growing number of persons interested in developing these abilities. Ongoing research at Metasource and other institutes will certainly expand the general awareness of these subjects.

"But the area of reincarnation demands immediate attention. People *are* experiencing *something*. They are viewing or reliving experiences which they believe are valid. And they are modifying their personal perspectives as a result. Many so-called 'ESP' experiences are difficult to capture or to define, but past-life recalls lend themselves to specific information and data which can be collected and analyzed. That is the beginning of verification."

I asked Shad if he would prepare a brief summary of some of the findings and case histories developed and researched during a year of seminars which Metasource sponsored in several major cities across the United States. Herewith is his report:

"What if reincarnation were an established fact, and everyone knew it?" This is a question often posed by the mystic and the student of the paranormal. Think of the difference it would make in the way people thought of one another, of themselves, and the world we live in today—and may have to reinhabit again a few years from now.

"It wouldn't be quite so easy to shrug off the ecologist's warnings," one reincarnation seminar attendee commented. "It's one thing to think that we can do whatever we want to Mother Earth and not have to worry about being around to pay the price. But when you think about coming back, living on the rubble of an abandoned open-strip mine, and boiling your own drinking water from a polluted river, that makes a difference. That makes it personal!"

Others who have relieved their own past lives feel that the implications would be far greater than just the effect on the physical environment. A young woman who was completing work for her doctorate in clinical psychology attended her second past-life age regression seminar both out of professional interest and a growing personal curiosity.

"I began to realize what would happen to our traditional concepts of human psychology if reincarnation became an accepted part of our reality," she explained. "For years we have been battling over which is more important, heredity or environment. Now we have a third influence to contend with—past lives! Maybe we've been looking for answers in the wrong places."

This young professional, like so many others, has started to look into past-life experiences for answers to many of today's questions. After reliving a number of her own previous incarnations, she can understand the impact this experience has on others.

"It's really true," she stated. "Once someone realizes that the original cause for some present problem lies in his or her own past, they seem to let go of it, and the problem starts to dissolve. We need to do a lot more study and follow-up, but this could be a breakthrough for modern psychology. Who would have thought that by the twenty-first century the biggest influence on modern psychology may not be Freud, or

Jung, or any of the others. It may be the rediscovery of a principle that is as old as man himself—reincarnation!"

We sponsor seminars because it is the most direct avenue for the input of information. If the institute ran an ad in a national magazine requesting personal past-life experiences, we would be deluged with ten- and twelve-page letters of interesting stories. But you can hardly program those into a computer.

We need specific facts—names, dates, incidents, details. By collecting data from seminar participants, and following up on that data, we can begin to verify the specifics and develop corollaries—similar pieces of information which tie together from widely divergent sources.

The research arm of The Metasource Institute which has the task of collecting and processing this mountain of information is The Metasource Research Society. The Society is made up of individual study groups located in cities throughout the United States. In each city where we have sponsored a past-life seminar or workshop, and in other cities where the interest is strong, we are offering individuals a chance to participate in the research work and have the opportunity to have their own past-life experiences researched.

As an example, if a woman in Houston, Texas, relives a lifetime as an eight-year-old boy in Seattle in 1857, with names, dates, and places, that is information which can be checked out. But, like other areas of paranormal research, few individuals have the time, money, or perhaps the inclination to fly to Seattle to undertake the difficult task of sifting through old records for the information. Our goal is to send an information form on any experience like this to the research group in that city for verifications. Once the information is researched, it will be forwarded to the institute for programming, and then on to the individual who made the request. In this way we can have a large number of research studies going on at the same time. The participants are sharing their time with others on a broad national scale, and they are able to obtain results that would otherwise not be possible.

Since members of the Metasource staff are in constant contact with hundreds of regression subjects and experiences, it would seem likely that we have taken the opportunity to explore personally their own past lives.

One of the most difficult things about this research is trying to maintain one's own objectivity. Many scientists fall into the trap of developing data to support their own biases. It is especially hard to maintain complete objectivity when you have had personal experiences which appear to be very valid.

As an example, at a past-life seminar in San Francisco, I saw myself in another lifetime, and it was very clear and believable. Especially when I noted that I saw or experienced things about which I had no previous conscious knowledge. And it is that area of "conscious knowledge" that we hope our research will clarify. If we are just tuning in to a universal unconscious, that alone would make the research well worthwhile—especially when you consider the impact of that concept on our traditional constructs of physics.

But many of the regression experiences are so detailed and specific that there is some reason to believe that it could be an actual personal experience which specifically relates to the person who is viewing it rather than randomly "tuning in" to some data bank of human experiences that are forever impressed on the "ethers" surrounding the planet.

During the regression at the San Francisco seminar, we were directed, while in hypnosis, to go back to the lifetime just previous to the one we are now living. Dick Sutphen was the hypnotist, and he very carefully guided us back, making sure that we could consciously, at any time, release ourselves and bring ourselves back to the present.

Dick told us to go to a day in that lifetime which was very important to that life experience. I found myself in an empty classroom at a college in New England. I was a teacher, and I was standing looking out of the window at the scene outside. The year was 1942, and it was early fall. I watched the cars on the street and I was very sad. I was wondering if we would ever see armored tanks and jeeps filing down that street, bringing the very real World War into that beautiful New England town.

Dick's voice guided quietly on in the background. My conscious mind remained alert and aware. Intellectually, I questioned why I should have chosen this particular day. It didn't seem to be very important. I felt a strong feeling of despair, but I couldn't seem to relate it to anything specific.

I left the classroom and walked slowly down the hallway. Every detail was crystal clear—the colors of the walls, the bookshelves, the aging linoleum on the floor, the high ceilings and windows with small-paned glass and dark varnished frames. It was that clarity that first made me realize that this experience was neither a dream nor a typical fantasy.

At the end of the hall I saw the doors to the old elevator. The concrete frame and cowling were designed with the familiar scrolls and sculpture which adorned so many buildings in the 1920s and 1930s. I still had that sad feeling of loss or despair as I pushed the elevator button and leaned against the frame waiting for the doors to slide open. I remember that I wasn't even surprised or startled when the doors opened and I stepped in and fell toward the bottom of the empty elevator shaft. The elevator wasn't there.

The reason for the lack of surprise or fear became immediately apparent to me. As I fell, I felt my "other" self slip effortlessly out of my physical body. "I" never hit the bottom. The physical body did, but that was no longer important. It didn't make any difference. In this lifetime, Shad was born in late September 1942.

Other members of the Metasource staff also experienced regressions. It was important to them as homework for their understanding and their research. But one young man, who was only indirectly involved with the past-life seminars, decided to find out for himself. Gregory Helmstetter is my nine-year-old son, and he visited a past-life seminar in Las Vegas in the spring of 1977.

A few teen-aged persons received special permission from time to time to attend a seminar with one or both of their parents. Atlhough children offer some of the best documented cases of reincarnation experiences, little work has been done with children using hypnosis on a group basis, and no one Gregory's age had ever attended one of the seminars.

Without stopping to ask, Gregory quietly took a position under a covered table at the back of the regression room. He rested comfortably on his pillow (borrowed from his room at the Sahara Hotel), and settled back unnoticed, to see what this was all about.

Later, after the regression, Gregory crawled out from under the table with a handwritten recap of his experience. It is interesting to note that Gregory was not told where he would be or what he would see. He, along with the rest of the seminar group, had only been told that they would be moved back into a time in the past.

Without questioning whether his experience was real or not, Gregory had trusted his mind and his memory.

"I'm in a room. It's a candleshop," Gregory wrote. "Me and my wife are in it. She is over at the old iron stove, and I'm eating something for a snack. On the window is a sign like this. [Here Gregory drew a detail of the sign in the window of the candleshop.]

"The front door is open and there are worn rounded-side-and-corner bricks for pavement. Many jugs and bottles with many different colored things inside of them. And they are all over many shelves. I was about forty-one years old. There is a yellow mist in the room, but very faint. My wife wore a long yellow and white dress. She had brown hair with a bun in it.

[At this point the group was directed to move forward to a later time in that same life.]

"It is some celebration, like Thanksgiving, but not Thanksgiving. My wife and I are there, and the two older people and one child younger than mine. There are two long tables (no turkey) not picnic tables; but the seats are joined with the table."

At this point, the group was brought back to the present, and out of hypnosis, being directed to remember everything they had experienced. Like so many persons who experience past-life regression, Gregory had brought back with him an astounding number of crystal-clear details, too numerous for him to write down in the dim light under the table where he was lying.

He remembered in vivid detail the wax drippings on the stone floor, the clasps and hinges on the window-panes and shutters, the way everything was placed in the room, and who his customers were. A vivid imagination could account for this scene; but again, this experience was viewed with the kind of clarity that memory supplies and fantasies seldom offer. There was no excitement in the scenes to add that certain "entertainment quality" to the mind of this nine-year-old boy—just the simple, clear memory of what he believed to be an actual experience.

Another Metasource member, Jean, a pretty woman in her thirties, believed that she could not be hypnotized. She had tried during several regressions but she was getting little more than vague impressions, not lucid images. Jean has always claimed that she does not think in pictures or graphic images, but rather in feelings and nonvisual impressions.

While discussing her concern about being a good hypnosis subject with semilan host Grant Gudmundson, Grant suggested that Jean have an individual regression, rather than continue to try unsuccessfully in a group situation. Jean stayed very busy during the seminars with registrations and hotel details, and Grant believed that it may be the tension of her seminar responsibilities that was keeping her from relaxing enough to go into hypnosis.

A private session was scheduled, and Grant set up his recorder while I and another Metasource member monitored. Jean got comfortable and waited for Grant to begin his slow, gentle countdown and conditioning that would take her into the hypnotic state. Minutes later, muscle by muscle, her entire body relaxed into deep hypnosis, and Grant began to move her back in time.

Grant directed Jean to go back to a time that was affecting her present lifetime in some way, to explore it, and understand its full meaning. Jean's face changed perceptibly, as she became not another woman in some past time, but a man, a seaman who, it soon became obvious, was not engaged in a life of spiritual good.

Jean found herself a buccaneer leading a life of some adventure and some hardships as well. Though not at all like the Hollywood portrayal of the exciting life of the high seas, it was a lifetime that proved to be important to Jean in her present life.

As a seaman, Jean experienced being tried and convicted of killing a shipmate while drunk. The punishment was painful and unforgettable. The seaman's right arm was tied by a rope to a post, and he was swung around the post until the muscles and ligaments of his arm were pulled and torn. This was to serve as a lesson to those who would let drinking and drunkenness lead them to harming another member of the crew. The seaman would be able to work again, but he would never forget the lesson. Never may have proved to have been a long time.

There is an interesting follow-up to Jean's story. During her present lifetime, Jean drinks very little. She has always believed that if you drink to excess you could do something wrong and get punished for it. For the past sixteen years, any time that Jean has sat at a table at a lounge or a restaurant and ordered a glass of spirits (particularly rum!), she has begun to get uncomfortable. If she remains, she will soon begin to feel pain and discomfort, and unconsciously reaches for her right shoulder. She will often wince with the discomfort which centers in her neck and right shoulder muscles. After she pushes the glass away or leaves the room, the discomfort will slowly go away.

Jean has tried to reason many times that it is the height of the table, the way she is seated, or the hour of the day. But none of these seem to have any effect when Jean is sipping coffee or a soft drink. Not until one day following a past-life regression did she realize that there could be quite another reason for the pain and discomfort.

Today Jean continues to drink very sparingly. She still believes that too much strong drink is best left to someone else. But she has not since reached for her shoulder at a table or felt the pain. Until Jean's regression into a past life, she may have unconsciously needed the reminder. But perhaps once the lesson became clear, she can now do without the painful reminder of one unfortunate incident in a past life.

CHAPTER TWENTY:
THE GOAL OF REBIRTH

"After years now of total involvement with past-life regression work, including the in-depth regressions of hundreds of individuals and the group regressions of thousands in seminars, metaphysical groups, colleges, and so forth, I still cannot say for certain exactly what I believe reincarnation to be," Dick Sutphen honestly admitted to me.

"In my opinion, several possibilities should be considered, and there is no way to know which concept is totally correct. Reality may be a combination of the concepts—or something we have yet to discover."

Here, by way of concluding this present volume, Dick Sutphen is sharing his own concepts, together with his interpretations of the theories of other researchers, which deal with the eternal promise of rebirth:

SPIRITUAL LINEAGE CONCEPT

You are who you are. You have never been anyone else, and you will never be anyone else. Yet you carry in your subconscious mind the spiritual essence of others who have lived before you. When you are hypnotically regressed into a previous lifetime, you are actually reliving the life of your creator.

As an example, in regression you see yourself as an Englishman in 1850. The man actually lived and died in that time period; and after crossing over into the nonphysical realms, he created you as an extension of his own identity to further explore Earth incarnations. His "spiritual essence" was introduced into you when you were but a fetus; thus, you are an extension of him. He is not controlling you, for once anything is created it is freed; but rather he is feeling and experiencing everything through you. His Karma, good and bad, is your Karma. His soul will continue to evolve, just as discussed in the classic concept, but for this nonphysical, detached perspective. When you cross over to the other side, you will have the same opportunity to experience through others of your own creation.

The Englishman may have fused his essence into several other individual entities at the same time. These other people would be your "counterparts" or "parallel-selves." This introduces the idea of simultaneous multiple incarnation, which I will talk about next.

SIMULTANEOUS MULTIPLE INCARNATIONS

The frequency of the Earth is accelerating; and as it does, more and more "old souls" will cross over as bodies become available. These souls are very experienced and have the ability to inhabit more than one body at a time. They seek to accelerate the evolutionary process by exploring as many lives as possible within the shortest time frame. It may be that, as the population of the world grows larger, it is actually growing smaller from a "soul count perspective." In other words, there are fewer souls, but as the frequencies continue to intensify, it will be the highly advanced souls who cross over to inhabit ever larger numbers of bodies at the same time.

If this concept is valid, you are only a part of your totality, with all of your "parallel-selves" comprising the whole soul. (This concept also explains the population explosion better than the Atlantis, Mu theory.)

LACK OF TIME CONCEPT

There is no such thing as time, and all of your lives—past, present, and future—are being lived at the same moment. Each historic period exists on the Earth within a different frequency of Time/Space, and thus each is invisible and untouchable to the others. Time would only relate to your perception, or possibly from your birth up until this moment.

If this concept is valid your past lives are affecting you, but you are also affecting your past lives, as you perceive the past. The same is true, of course, for the future.

This concept can be combined with any of the others I've mentioned. It is also in keeping with several scientific theories, including one of Einstein's.

THE OVERSOUL CONCEPT

The very essence of your soul is existing as an "Oversoul" on the other side, possibly on a Godhead level. Physical lifetimes are lived as a form of procreation and expansion of the Oversoul energy. You are like a cell in the body of your God-level totality—the part and the whole at the same time. This concept is compatible with any of the previous mentioned concepts.

The Oversoul could conceivably be exploring within billions of potentials at the same time.

To better understand the part-and-whole concept, think of a single cell within your body. It contains your complete "pattern." If our human cloning abilities were developed, as they are with some reptiles, you could be "duplicated" from that cell. Projecting the concept from a superconscious level, you have all of the knowledge of your Oversoul, or God totality. That knowledge may be existing within the ninety-five percent of mind that is not normally used.

THE TOTAL ILLUSION CONCEPT

Life is an illusionary game, created as an evolutionary process for the Soul—or maybe—simply for the fun of it. You are God. You created the entire environment (world) to make the game seem real and to give you limitless possibilities of exploration. Maybe everybody else actually exists, but maybe they are only illusions.

In a hypnotic trance the hypnotized subject can often "totally relive" a past situation. His voice becomes that of a five year old, and he relives a traumatic situation just as realistically as he did the first time at the age of five. From this perspective, your life could be a self-created hypnoticlike illusion.

THE CLASSIC CONCEPT

Reincarnation is an evolving process of physical exploration for the perfection of the soul, a system of total justice and balance. We learn needed lessons through

Karma (cause and effect) and carry this intuitive knowledge with us through successive incarnations. Each entity is born into each new Earth life with a level of awareness (vibrational rate) established in his past lives. How the lifetime is lived will dictate whether the rate is raised or lowered.

In the nonphysical realms of "the other side" there are seven levels. Each successive level is more desirable, with the top level being the God-level, or Godhead. It is our vibrational rate which dictates our level after death. The entity, upon crossing over, will seek the level of his own rate, but will be unable to remain in the more intense upper levels.

Due to our desire to perfect our Soul, and thus to return to the Godhead, we reincarnate into successive Earth lives in hopes of using our past-life knowledge to live a "good" physical life. In so doing, we will raise our vibrational rate, moving closer to our "soul-goal" of returning to God.

Although he is not dogmatic in his definition of what reincarnation may be, Dick Sutphen is completely convinced that that which we perceive as the past is somehow affecting the present.

I agree that regardless of how reincarnation is viewed philosophically, it would appear that certain of our past lives are affecting our present life.

In some multilevel, spiritual way, our essential selves, our Souls, will be born again to grow and to evolve to the Greater Essence from whence they came.

Once we have pondered the importance of our past lives, we must transform the present into a meaningful growth experience and in this manner prepare ourselves for as significant a future as possible.

* * *

"Isn't it odd," Francie remarked, "that whenever we speak of reincarnation we automatically think of past lives? Actually, reincarnation, rebirth, suggests the future in an existence yet to come.

"Science teaches us that Nature continually evolutionizes humankind so as to perpetuate its most prized species," she continued. "Is it Mother Nature alone whose fingers manipulate the adaptability of mankind? Have we not enough evidence to indicate that the existence of mankind is not merely an evolutionary happenstance of Nature?

"Throughout Earth's many ages, our Souls have been incarnating into the realm of matter, gaining the higher vibrations of Love, Wisdom, and Knowledge through experience for the sole purpose of one day ascending to the realm from which they fell. The Soul is thereby evolutionizing on the spiritual plane as human life evolutionizes on the physical plane, for the material plane is merely the outer manifestation of that which is occurring on the nonmaterial plane.

"We are now in the dawning of a New Age in which spiritual laws will apply. *Remember:* 'On Earth as it is in Heaven.' A fast-approaching spiritual and societal transformation will soon change both the physical and the psychical structure of our planet, affecting as well the evolution of our Souls and their many lifetimes.

"No one should wish to be left behind in this coming evolution of mankind and that of his Soul. Those of sensitivity will welcome an opportunity to link up with the New Age before the Earth's coming dramatic change. We must prepare ourselves to become positive—the 'sheep' of the New Age, rather than the 'goats' that will perish. Will your Soul incarnate as one of the sheep? Perhaps you might ask yourself the following questions:

"Are you willing to vibrate with the frequencies of Love, Wisdom, and Knowledge and give of these highest energies to those around you?

"Are you ready to dedicate yourself to the spiritual laws of peace and harmony?

"Can you truly say that you love all that carries the life force of creation?

"Each individual who wishes to assist his or her Soul in its future incarnation so as to insure its survival as a 'sheep' must now begin practicing the ideal of living that will be a part of the New Age. He or she must vibrate with the highest frequencies of Love, Wisdom, and Knowledge and give of these energies to the betterment of others. Each person must bcome balanced in perspective and view all things both realistically and idealistically. Everyone must learn to respect all life around him, human, animal, and plant.

"You must learn to sublimate your ego to that of your Soul, your Higher Self, the Hierarchy," Francie went on. "You must become an instrument of your Soul.

"The more positive you become, the more easily you will attain the highest vibrations of Love, Wisdom, and Knowledge. Possessing these, you will reflect more of your Soul, thereby fulfilling the purpose of your birth and assisting the joining of your Soul with the Hierarchy.

"Energizing yourself with Love attunes yourself to the realm of higher vibrations. In this way you will increasingly be able to draw upon the positive forces that come from Heaven. As you accelerate your evolution, you will progress out of your old physical limitations into a new understanding and thereby gain the wisdom that is yours by right of your cosmic inheritance. You will then make ready your Soul's rebirth on Earth, its reincarnation in the New Age.

"But the gaining does not cease here. Upon the cessation of your present life you will become incorporated into your Soul and be prepared to ascend with it when it returns to the Hierarchal realm. You will be ready for your most important birth—your *Starbirth!*"